the 9 WEEK MIRACLE

the 9 WEEK MIRACLE

A Son's Incredible Survival Story

MARYANNE SHAW

NEW YORK

the 9 WEEK MIRACLE
A Son's Incredible Survival Story

ISBN 978-1-61448-355-7 paperback
ISBN 978-1-61448-356-4 eBook
Library of Congress Control Number: 2012945362

Morgan James Publishing
The Entrepreneurial Publisher
5 Penn Plaza, 23rd Floor
New York City, New York 10001
(212) 655-5470 office • (516) 908-4496 fax
www.MorganJamesPublishing.com

Cover Design by:
Rachel Lopez
www.r2cdesign.com

Interior Design by:
Bonnie Bushman
bonnie@caboodlegraphics.com

In an effort to support local communities, raise awareness and funds, Morgan James Publishing donates a percentage of all book sales for the life of each book to Habitat for Humanity Peninsula and Greater Williamsburg.

Get involved today, visit
www.MorganJamesBuilds.com.

DEDICATION

For my dear son Nick and his beautiful wife,
Hallie: For all you are and all you are meant to be.
I love you with all my heart. Mom

CONTENTS

INTRODUCTION

Have you ever gotten a phone call that changed your life? To be fair, sometimes those kinds of calls can be good news. They're engaged! Surgery was a success! The baby was born! You got the job! But some of those calls are anything but good news. That was the kind of phone call I received on Tuesday, July 27, 2010 at 4:53 PM

From our Blog: Wednesday, July 28, 2010 10:30 PM, EDT

On July 27, 2010 at about 4:30 PM Nick was in his open garage using a workshop vacuum to clean up sawdust in his boat after working on replacing the floorboards. He had emptied the gas out of the tank and actually removed the tank from the boat. But the gas tank itself remained in the garage. There were gas fumes that ignited causing a vapor explosion, which led to the boat's gas tank exploding. Nick heard the boom, and felt himself being assisted off the side of the boat to a narrow space on the concrete floor of the garage. Smoldering, he ran out and dove into their inflatable swimming pool. He remembers running into the house, retrieving his phone and attempting to call 9-1-1. Realizing he was burned, he went and sat on his front lawn. The

Greentown Fire Department responded within minutes, and Nick was transported to the Akron Children's Hospital Burn Unit.

Nick suffered burns over 46% of his body. The most serious were those to his legs, feet, shoulders, arms and hands. He also has some burns to his face and chest but not as serious as the others. He has a long recovery time ahead of him, and your thoughts and prayers are welcomed and appreciated.

Nick is a loving, generous guy and a bright star in the life of his family, friends and all who know him. He is already a favorite here in the Burn Unit and has a wonderful attitude. God and his angels were definitely watching out for him. We are grateful he is alive!

Nick's Mom

What follows, is not only the account of what happened but also the testament of so many lives that were affected. You'll hear in Nick's words about his angelic encounter at the peak of the crisis. Nick's courage and attitude have proven to be an inspiration to so many. This was a life-changing event, in more ways than one…

I have always believed that everything in this life happens for a reason. This is no exception. Let's start on this journey together as I take you through The Nine-Week Miracle…

THE ROAD TO THE 9-WEEK MIRACLE

1

What follows are the excerpts from our blog and my journal that I maintained throughout the ordeal. Sometimes the words in my personal journal will repeat a little of what was posted to my online blog, but with greater detail. Also included are some of the messages from friends and loved ones. What better way to express the facts and emotions from that time then through the words of the moment...

From my Journal, Wednesday, July 28, 2010 1:30 PM

Sitting in Nick's hospital room watching my baby try to get some sleep amidst the pain he is in...

Yesterday, Tuesday, July 27, 2010, about 4:30 PM, he was using a workshop vacuum to sweep up sawdust after replacing some floorboards in his boat. There must have been some gas fumes in the air (even though Nick had pulled out the gas tank) causing a spark to go back to the source and the boat's gas tank exploded. Nick heard the boom and immediately felt assistance as he dove off the side of the boat, as though diving into water, onto a narrow space on the concrete garage floor. He escaped from the garage though he recalls looking up to see if the orange flames were above him. Running around the outside of the garage, he dove into a small inflatable swimming pool that he had just bought at a garage sale. Oh how I had teased him for this purchase!

After jumping out of the pool, Nick ran into the house, got his phone and called 9-1-1. At least he thought he dialed it, in reality he just hit a bunch of numbers. He went back outside and sat down on the grass in his front yard. At that point he knew he was burnt because the breeze hurt!

A neighbor heard the boom and came running over. He moved Nick's red truck away from the garage reducing the damage it sustained. He also called 9-1-1 and sat with Nick until the emergency crew arrived.

I was speaking to my son, David, on the phone at about 4:50 PM as I was leaving church. As we were talking and he was nearing his home which is near Nick's house, he noticed black smoke. He remembers the strange thought that crossed his mind, "I hope Nick's garage isn't on fire!" Just then he noticed a call coming in from Nick's wife, Hallie, and he told me he had to take that call.

I pulled into my garage, changed clothes and started to prepare dinner when Hallie called me. She said "Are you home?" I answered, "Yes." She cried out "There's a fire at our house and Nick is burnt!" I exclaimed, "Oh my God! I'll go there right now!" She continued, "I talked to David, and he is there. He talked to Nick; and he said he is walking around, but I'm nervous." I assured her that I would go right over and call her back. I grabbed my purse, phone and keys and tore out the door.

I sped over there. I called my husband, Skip, as I was driving (not the best idea) and told him what had happened. He immediately said he'd meet me there, he was about 10 minutes away. I remember scanning the sky for smoke. As I approached his house I saw emergency vehicles. I pulled onto his lawn and limped as fast as my leg cast from my broken ankle would allow me. I was horrified at the blackened shell of the third bay of the garage, which had housed the boat. I headed there, forgetting that Nick had been outside walking around.

Two firemen headed toward me with arms up as I said, "This is my son!" They told me "He is on his way to Akron Children's Hospital." I choked out "How is he?" They answered, "He's burned pretty good". I was shaking so badly at this point as I asked for directions to the hospital. The firemen gently told me that I needed to have somebody drive me there. I mumbled that my husband was on his way.

Just then I saw my son, David, who tried to reassure me. I knew I wouldn't rest until I saw him with my own eyes. The firemen told David not to allow me to drive anywhere, and he took my keys. It seemed like forever for Skip to get there and for us to get to the hospital. We had to stop for gas, which took what seemed like a very long time. On the way I was in contact with Hallie by phone. She was making her way to Akron from Medina in rush hour traffic on unfamiliar roads. She was unsure of her directions and I tried to help keep her calm.

Once we did arrive at the ER, a valet parked our car and we rushed in. We were brought right in and told Nick had been taken to the Burn Unit. They gave us a series of directions on how to get to the burn unit that sounded like gibberish to me. The hospital chaplain was there and must have seen the distress on our faces. He offered to take us to the Burn Unit. He kindly did that and situated us in the waiting room just outside the Burn Unit itself. I then asked him to go to the ER to escort the pretty blonde who would be arriving shortly, Nick's wife. He hurried off to the ER. Shortly after, he returned with Hallie.

Then the nurse came in and filled us in on Nick's condition. He had suffered serious burns of what they estimated covered 46% of his body. He was burned on his hands, fingers, arms, shoulders, legs and feet. They said he was wearing a tank top and shorts and didn't think he was burnt under there and had only minor burns on his face. They were getting ready to put him in a special tub, cut off the dead skin and dress the wounds. We could expect one day in the hospital for every one per cent of burn to the body, at least 46 days. That was if everything was perfect with no infection, no skin graft surgery and no nutrition issues. We were reeling! Good nutrition would be vital to his skin healing. He would have three days to try to eat 4000 calories a day before they would put in a feeding tube. She said we could come see him for a minute.

We walked back, and there he sat in a bed completely draped expect for his head. He looked like he was in pain. The first thing he said was "Somebody is going to have to do my work." I assured him I would handle it. I kissed his head before I left him and told him I loved him as did Skip. Hallie and Nick expressed their love and tenderness for each other, which is hard to do with minimal touching. The last thing he said before we left the room was "I'm sorry for worrying you." It was all I could do not to sob.

We were led out of the room so the grueling dressing process could begin. Hallie had to go to registration and I went along. When we came out, the chaplain magically appeared. Hallie seemed ready to collapse. He led us into the chapel where she broke down. She said, "He doesn't deserve this!" Which of course, he doesn't, he's such a great guy. But really, who does deserve something like this? I wouldn't wish it on anybody. I reminded Hallie how God and his angels had been with him because he was still alive! We stayed in the chapel for a little while and let our tears fall before we made our way back to the waiting room.

When Nick was wheeled past, he was bandaged everywhere except for his face and chest. He was pretty alert and remembered everything. Hallie and I went and got him some food from the cafeteria including chicken fingers, mozzarella sticks, potatoes and broccoli. He needed those calories!

A short bit later, a nurse said they needed to put a Foley™ in. He looked at me and said, "What's a Foley™?" I said, "Oh honey, it's a catheter." His eyes got as round as saucers. He wasn't happy. But I have to say Nick is so accepting of all of it, the catheter, the IV, the central line they had to put in when the IV fell out, this entire process. He said, "It's what I have to do to get better." He's quite a guy, my son. I love him dearly.

From our Blog: Wednesday, July 28, 2010 10:30 PM, EDT

A little over 24 hours has passed since the accident, and as Nick's mom I can tell you it is very hard to watch my youngest child lie in that bed in pain. I want to change places with him and take it all away from him, yet I cannot. His burns are worse than they thought. They think there are third degree burns on the legs and shoulders, and the doctor thinks he will need skin graft surgery in those areas in about a week and a half. Also, last night, his face was not bandaged and seemed to only have minor burns on his chin and nose, but the burns have come out there. Although they don't feel he will have scarring on his face, he does have burns there. They have wrapped his head completely in the dressing so he sort of resembles a mummy. Also, the other change from last night is the addition of the feeding tube today. Nick wasn't happy about that. He seemed up to the task to attempt to take in 4000 calories a day. Those of you that know him know that

Nick can eat! When they told him that they were going to put in a feeding tube, Nick sat straight up and said, "NO, I can eat 4000 calories!" But they explained it would speed healing and better his nutrition with the tube. After it was inserted, Nick's comment was "I'm not a fan." A classic Nick comment.

Nick has been very accepting of everything else throughout this ordeal thus far. From the IV's to the placement of a central line through and including the knowledge of daily dressing changes. Nick says it's what he has to do to get better. He has a great attitude. He's quite a man, my son. I love him. I thank God that he spared his life yesterday and sent his angels to protect him...

Nick's Mom

Wednesday, July 28, 2010 10:58 PM

Nick & Hallie, you're in our prayers and thoughts. Don't worry about anything else except getting through this. I would even root for the Browns for you if it would ease the pain you're going through. Stay strong. Love, Jimmy

Jimmy DiCola

Wednesday, July 28, 2010 11:30 PM

Nick and family, we are sending prayers, love and continued wishes for the fastest recovery possible. Word is spreading fast and the prayers are just amazing. Our Lord protected you yesterday and will continue to do so. You have SO many people who love and care about you. We love you.

Cathy & Ronnie Hart

From our Blog: Thursday, July 29, 2010 3:28 PM, EDT

We are so encouraged today! First of all when we saw Nick first thing this morning, his face looked so much less swollen.

Hallie said that it was because they had stopped given him fluids through the IV, which would make him less swollen. He is drinking a lot on his own. SO he looks better. He is still bandaged from head to toe. Secondly, the doctor was in and they think that his hands are not as severely injured as initially thought so that is such great news! He estimates the first of his skin graft surgeries to be next week on his upper arm and left leg. They still need to determine where else they are needed. The skin will come from his upper legs and back, which weren't burned. The biggest encouragement is hearing that he could heal much quicker than we were told. I can't tell you the relief that news gave us! Of course we know that is barring complications but we are staying positive.

As always Nick is alert and talking and a wonderful guy. He does have lots of pain and is heavily medicated so he does fade in and out. He loves visitors. PLEASE if you have a cold or any kind of infection, don't come! But if you are healthy, a visit is good. Only two at a time are allowed and a gown is a must to keep out infection. That would be devastating at this juncture! We gather in the waiting room and take turns. Blessings to all of you who love Nick so dearly!!!

Nick's Mom

From my Personal Journal: Thursday, July 29, 2010

As I approached the parking deck, Hallie called to tell me that they had to put in a feeding tube to insure he got the calories he needed. They also wrapped his face and chest as burns had shown themselves. I was bawling as I pulled in, missing where you get the ticket. The agent had to get it for me. She was so sweet. I had to brace myself to see him all bandaged, just thinking about it made tears run down my cheeks.

I finally saw him and after the initial shock it was ok. His lips and eyelids looked swollen to me. Gosh, I'm so worried. I cannot stand to see him in pain. They are really very good here. But we have no control and I can't stand to see my baby hurting. I can't take it away from him although I would take it from him onto me in a heartbeat if I could. I cannot stand to see him suffer. Please God, give me the strength to face each day of this crisis.

He had lots of visitors yesterday, and they do cheer him. He will fade when he is tired. He is heavily medicated with Morphine®, Oxycontin® and Lord knows what else. And still he won't be pain free. We set up an online blog last night. I wrote the initial story and first entry when I got home on Wednesday. Then I emailed the link to everybody I could think of. When I got up today, the first thing I did was check the website. Already so many postings! I have so many postings from my family and friends! I am overwhelmed to be so cared about!

From our Blog: Thursday, July 29, 2010 11:06 PM, EDT

(Hallie) Today I met one of Nick's guardian angels... Nate Netti stopped by the house today while I was home for a quick shower. He informed me that while he was driving to work on Tuesday afternoon around 4:50PM he saw fire coming from our garage. He said that he realized that it must have just started because he could still see into the garage because the smoke had not blackened yet. He did not see anyone outside so he immediately ran towards the house to let "the owner" know that there was a fire. The next thing he knew he saw Nick running out of the house. He was burned and soaking wet from jumping in the pool. Nate immediately called 911. This call, in addition to Nick's quick sense to dive out of the boat and into the pool may have saved his life. I am so thankful to Nate because he was so caring to stop at a total strangers house and help. Also because the 9-1-1 call that Nick THOUGHT he made didn't go through! Nate ensured a quick emergency response.

Shortly after, he and two other men (who I think were our neighbors, Nick Bloomer and Matt Hamric) even thought to run in our house to look for our keys and move our cars. They were able to find Nick's keys and move his truck.

Everyone has left for the night. Nick is resting up for a tough week to come. The nurses came in tonight to tell us a little of what to expect next week when he has his surgeries. They said that he will be in a lot more pain than he is now because all of his nerves will be exposed. He is so strong. He didn't ask any questions or seem nervous. He just knows it has to be done to get better. He has been handling all of this so well keeping a great attitude. He is a wonderful, kind, hopeful, and strong man! He and I truly appreciate all of you that are visiting, thinking of him, praying for him, offering to help, and writing him these wonderful posts! I know that it is a huge part of why his spirits are so high! To ALL OF YOU, THANK YOU!!!

To my wonderful husband, I love you more every day. Get well soon!

Thursday, July 29, 2010 12:30 AM

Dear Nick, Hallie, Maryanne and Skip, On behalf of our immediate family and the entire Premier family we send our love and support!! We are here for you!! Anything, you just say the words and consider it done!!! That's what family is about right!! Seems like yesterday that we were dancing at Nick and Hallie's wedding...I look forward to the day we all dance again!! It will happen!!! All our Love,

Stephanie Green

Thursday, July 29, 2010 12:57 AM

Hey Nick, You and Hallie are constantly in my thoughts. I'm so sorry that you have to go through this much pain. You are the only person I know who could make it through this with a smile on their face. Keep working hard. We love you!

Karrie DeWalt

From our Blog: Friday, July 30, 2010 2:14 PM, EDT

OK, they told us this would be like a roller coaster ride. It looks like yesterday we had the thrill of coming down the hill and today we are climbing up. We found out that the original estimate of 46 days in the hospital was closer to correct. In fact, they think he is looking at around 50 days here in the hospital. Although when we first heard this on Tuesday when he was admitted we were totally shocked, but then we had wrapped our heads around that news. But after hearing it could be less, we were encouraged. Now having to go back to the longer time frame, well we feel a bit devastated again.

Then we talked to the doctor and learned that he does have chemical burns (caused from the gasoline) and it does take days for the full extent of the burns to show. It will take a few days more before we know for sure. Each day they tend to look worse. He is planning 3 skin graft surgeries for next week maybe even 4. Hallie and I asked a lot of questions and got a little ahead of where we need to be at this point. We even overwhelmed ourselves with the scope of what we were asking. The psychologist came in and talked to us and advised that we not try to deal with the whole thing just yet, but to concentrate on the immediate, which is the skin graft surgeries. Good advice, now if my mind will just take heed!

Nick was at a pain level of 7 this morning and asked for meds soon after I arrived around 9AM. He is so sweet when he asks. Wednesday he asked during shift change and it was taking a couple of minutes and he was squirming. I thought I was going to have to be like Shirley Maclaine in "Terms of Endearment" You know the scene..."GIVE MY DAUGHTER THE SHOT!!!" Don't think I won't do it...

I am sitting here right now watching him sleep. He had his dressing change later than normal today. He wasn't completely as medicated for it today and he remembers. We already told them to hike it up for tomorrow. Hallie is napping. I am feeling very emotional right now. But I do know this: I love Hallie so much for loving my son as much as she does. She is like a daughter to me and both Skip and I would do anything to help ease her hurting right now.

Thank you all so much for the total outpouring of love and support these posts are showing. It completely humbles me.

Love, Nick's Mom

From my Personal Journal: Friday, July 30, 2010

Thursday was a good day. We felt so encouraged because the occupational therapist said he may heal faster. She herself hadn't seen his burns, but since we liked her message, we were desperate to latch onto it. I posted to our blog and everyone was so excited. It was a good day. Nick taught me how to print the labels at his office too. He talked fast as he told me, trying to finish talking before he got a dose of pain meds. I wrote notes like crazy, so I sure hope I can decipher them!

Today now is Friday, July 30th. They warned us about the roller coaster ride of the Burn Unit. Yesterday we had the thrill of coming down the hill, but today we are going back up the hill. The day started with my phone ringing at 7:03 AM. I looked at the display and it said Nick! I about had a heart attack. He wanted to tell me he had been awake early and had been thinking. He had decided that rather than having different people coming in to help at his business at random times doing the mail, he wanted to see if the couple that used to help him, Cora and Dean, could handle it. They were familiar with it and could come in each morning so things could get done as usual. Nick: the practical one with the cool business head even now.

As I drove to Nick's office to attempt the printing of the labels, I called Cora. She was more than happy to agree. I successfully printed (Yea!) and then went to the hospital, which was only a short distance away from his office location. Once there I found out he was having his bath at 11 AM instead of 8 AM, which kind of threw things off a bit. Since he'd been up extra early, he slept in the morning, not getting to eat. Then during his bath he wasn't medicated enough and felt too much, was in a lot of pain.

When he got back to his bed, Hallie observed his wounds alongside the Doctor, Doctor McCollum. Since he was exposed and has no skin, he was shivering uncontrollably. Hallie couldn't stand that and asked that they cover him and she left the room.

The news today was discouraging. We had been told upon admittance to expect one day for each 1 per cent of burns. So, 46 per cent equals 46 days. We were shocked when we heard that but began to wrap our heads around it. The staff keeps saying that his burns are a work in progress, and that fifty days is a good estimate.

Friday, July 30, 2010 10:52 AM

Hello Nick and all your loving family, we are thinking of you and truly admire your positive attitude! You are a STRONG man in many ways and this will excel your recovery! We are thrilled to hear the good news your mom posted yesterday!! I admire your mom for so many qualities...her strength, resilience, perseverance and just her "NO QUIT" attitude...you have definitely inherited those admirable traits!!! We are praying for all of you!! Love, Stephanie, Rob & girls

Stephanie Green

Friday, July 30, 2010 1:58 PM

Dear Maryanne and family, I am so sorry to hear that you got some bad news today. My heart is breaking for all of you. I hope that you know that there just isn't one guardian angel looking after Nick, but many!! He will pull thru this even if it takes longer than you thought. I wish there was something I could do to comfort you and Hallie. I hope you do find some comfort knowing we are all praying for Nick as hard as we can and won't stop! I know that your head must be swirling with all that is going on, but please try to do what the Dr. said and just concentrate on one thing at a time. Once that thing is over, you will feel like you have made a step forward! Nick must be such a strong young man to go thru this like he is. Please let him know that we are all thinking of him and wishing him nothing but a speedy recovery. It will happen! Love you, Adrienne

Adrienne Dawes

Friday, July 30, 2010 4:54 PM

I was on a plane heading to New York when I read the newspaper story about the accident. Later, when I received the email from Maryanne and learned it was you, it was like a blow to the stomach. It is devastating to have this happen to someone you love. The outpouring of love and support in these posts is a real tribute to the man you have become. I know that the path to recovery will be long and difficult, but I also know that you will travel that path with courage. You have a lot of people praying for you. Hang in there. Love, Uncle Lee

Lee DiCola

From our Blog: Saturday, July 31, 2010 11:50 AM, EDT

Hallie and I just spoke to the doctor as Nick is finishing up his bath and daily dressing change. He said the burns look about the same today maybe even more favorable than yesterday. We hold onto that with thanksgiving, we need that! He further explained that burns tend to change appearance daily and he has to re-evaluate daily. He knows the skin graft surgery is on for next week, but the how many and the where is uncertain at this time. We will take the small encouragements with happiness knowing to guard against anything that will cause the BIG LETDOWN such as we had the other day.

Last night his head bandages fell completely forward and they had to take them off. How nice it was to see his whole head and face today! His face looks red and peeled but not too bad. We were hoping he could keep the wraps off, and the doctor said YES! Thank you Lord! So now we get to see his beautiful, handsome face. It feels like a small step forward.

He had to start breathing treatments yesterday, 10 times an hour when he is awake. They are watching his respiration to guard against pneumonia. I guess I am a little annoying in reminding Nick about this. But if his respiration gets too low they will have to put in a respirator. They had told me that up front as a potential risk. I don't want that to happen, so I am a little like a police dog on this issue. Nick told me, "Mom, don't tell me I have to do in 10 minutes. Don't tell me I have to do it in 5 minutes. Just tell me when it's time to do it, and I'll do it!" Point taken.

The visits to this site blow me away! The posts are so uplifting. Thank you all so much. Thank you doesn't even say what is in my heart, Hallie's heart, all of our hearts. I love you all...

Nick's Mom

Saturday, July 31, 2010 2:47 AM

"To one who has faith, no explanation is necessary. To one without faith, no explanation is possible." St Thomas Aquinas.[1] We love you Nick! Get Well Soon!

Karrie DeWalt

Saturday, July 31, 2010 9:49 AM

Dear AMA, Nick, Hallie — Our hearts break for all of you and we are offering prayers every day. Hard to understand why something like this could happen to a guy like Nick. That which we can't understand is difficult to accept. I guess that's where faith comes into play, and what examples Grandma and Grandpa set for all of us. I picture Grandma's tears from heaven and Grandpa consoling her and trying to tell us that this is all going to be ok. Hallie, the way AMA described the way you love Nick reminds me of Grandma and Grandpa and the way they loved and cared for each other. I don't think I've ever likened anyone to them before. Picture DiColas' both near and far with arms stretched out and hands clasped tightly, creating a strong circle around you to protect you. 50 days...should we consider a fundraiser to help

---

1   St Thomas Aquinas quote, http://www.brainyquote.com/quotes/authors/t/thomas_aquinas_4.html

offset hospital expenses? I am happy to organize that if needed. Much Love, Cherie & Family

Cherie Grescovich

***Note**: AMA is the moniker Cherie has always used with me. It stands for Aunt Maryanne*

Saturday, July 31, 2010 10:53 AM

Dear Aunt Maryanne, Nick, Hallie, Reading about your feelings of being overwhelmed reminded me of this: "Because of the Lord's great love we are not consumed, for His compassions never fail. They are new every morning; great is your faithfulness" (Lam 3:2223) [2]

One day at a time is good advice – remember that God gives us enough grace to get through today. Nick, hang in there. You (and your family) are in my prayers every day. Aunt Maryanne – your love and gratitude, shine through your journal entries, it is lovely. It is a testimony to your faith and to the One in whom your faith lies. Love, Ellen

Ellen Cooper

Saturday, July 31, 2010 12:56 PM

Dear Nick, I still can't believe that this terrible thing has happened to you. I will be praying for you along with a long list of others. I will light a candle for you on Sunday. I hope your pain eases as the days pass. The following prayer was one that I found when my brother was sick:

God, give me the eyes to see your face in the midst of my troubles. Thank you for never leaving me and for giving me what I need to persevere through my roughest days. Amen [3]

---

2   The Holy Bible: Lamentations 3:2223
3   Devotions, Hope for the Hurting, Archives for 6/14/07, soulrehab.org, Joel Osteen, http://soulrehab.org/thejourney/index.php?m=20070614

P.S Eye of the Tiger

Dear MA & Hallie, Please remember to take care of yourselves so that you will be able to help Nick.

Monica Witmer

From our Blog: Sunday, August 1, 2010 11:34 AM, EDT

Hello to our loving support system! Today is Nick and Hallie's 2nd Anniversary. Think for a second what we were all doing two years ago today. A happy, joyous day. There will be many, many more happy days ahead for this couple who are so in love! They will get there and all of us will help them, one step at a time.

Big news today. At first there was no real change. He got his bath and dressing change a little earlier today, which is a good thing. They had him take the few steps, with assistance, to the little fold up cart that wheels him to the whirlpool bath. It was hard for him, but he did it. Movement is so important.

His face continues to improve. When the doctor first came in, we did ask about his respiration saturation level. He is on oxygen now. The oxygen helps him. He has been doing his breathing exercises like a champ! The doctor says he isn't worried about his respiration now, and he does not think he will have to go on a respirator. I went weak-kneed at that news as I was mentally trying to prepare myself for it just in case.

The doctor came back in about an hour later and had decided to move up the first of the skin graft surgeries to MONDAY. It will be his entire right arm. Still not sure about the hands. The doctor said he will be able to tell once he is in surgery if the hands need a graft or not. The skin will be taken from the upper leg for this surgery. Surgery will be at 9AM and will last until about noon. They will take him earlier for his bath and peel. Following surgery he will go to recovery.

I am glad to move on to this next stage as it means progress, yet anxious too. My other two children have been champions in strength. David was a rock at the scene of the accident. He handled everything there with a clear head starting with me who careened up to the scene in my car just after Nick was carried off in the ambulance. He has dealt with the filing of the initial claims and insurance adjusters and so many, many details. I learned just how well he can handle a crisis. I am so proud of him. Marcy was in Cincinnati on business when she got the call and had to drive here alone the following day. She has dealt with many details to help in this crisis. Her help also invaluable. My husband Skip, has had to stay away from the hospital until this coming Tuesday because he is healing from a staph infection on his leg. His antibiotics will be completed on Tuesday and his doctor and the burn unit cleared him to come in then. He is an enormous source of strength for me, and I know how hard it has been for him to have to stay away. But he loves Nick and only wants the absolute best for him, of course. And Hallie, she is his most loving wife. She is such a source of encouragement for him! Gosh how they love each other!

We will post tomorrow as soon as we know something after the surgery. Right now what is running through my head is this... God please grant me the serenity to accept the things I cannot change, courage to change the things I can, and wisdom to know the difference....Reinhold Niebuhr [4]

Nick's Mom

Sunday, August 1, 2010 4:21 PM

Dear uncle nick I hope you feel better. I will play with brody until you get home. I miss you. Love ruby

Ruby DeWalt, Age 6

---

4   Serenity Prayer, Reinhold Niebuhr: http://en.wikipedia.org/wiki/Serenity_Prayer

Sunday, August 1, 2010 4:35 PM

Dear unkle nick I miss you. Did the chlorine help you or not? Are all the nurses nice? Did you crall to the pool? Did you cry? I would. Does it hurt now? How do you get up too go to the bathroom? When are you going to take the bandages off your arms and legs? I hope you are feeling better soon. I love you. Love grace

Grace DeWalt, Age 8

Sunday, August 1, 2010 10:53 PM

Nick, I am awestruck by your strength. You are the ultimate hero in my eyes as you take each day with incredible will and determination. Please know that I am thinking of you and praying for you as you undergo your first surgery. I am so sorry that I cannot be there, but my heart certainly is. I love you! Marcy

Marcy DeWalt

From our Blog: Monday, August 2, 2010 1:24 PM, EDT

Quick update! The surgeon just came out; he made it through the first surgery! He said that the burns were deep, but it went well. Today they put the grafts all down his shoulder, arm, and back of the hand....more to follow

Nick's Mom

From our Blog: Monday, August 2, 2010 5:32 PM, EDT

Oh my gosh, this has been an emotional day. This is going to be a very tough week, let me just say that from the start. They told us this week would be very painful for him, but I don't think I really got it until Hallie and I saw him after the surgery in the recovery room. We are both glad the process has started, and we know and understand that it is necessary to go through this for the healing to begin; but it is SO HARD to see him in pain. He was still pretty doped up when I left to go and write this post. They did the graft to his entire right arm including shoulder and fingers but not the palm. The doctor said it was a hard surgery, but he is a young, healthy guy. They took the skin from his right leg and partial chest area. We were told those wounds would be more painful than the burn wounds.

They will do the exact same surgery tomorrow on the left arm. He needs an enormous amount of rest to heal and I just hope they can keep his pain levels down to tolerable levels. They didn't give him a pain pump, which was all he was talking about before he went in this morning. I can only guess it's because as he keeps having additional surgery and the pain increases in intensity they will give him the pain pump at that time and it will seem like blessed relief then.

From a health standpoint, he will recover and this will become a dim memory. I believe everything, including every hardship we have to bear, happens to us for a reason, even though we don't always know what that reason is. Sometimes how we handle our hardships inspires others, sometimes it brings opportunities our way that we never dreamed. Countless things can happen and do. But it is hard to think of things like that when going through a crisis. But the doctor told us he will recover! It may be slow, but he will recover!

As a mom I am having a hard time standing seeing his pain, but know I have to be strong for him. I actually left the hospital for a bit to write this post. It is tearing me up. My head knows this too shall pass but my heart says JUST STOP IT NOW!!!

I also know that God sees the little sparrow fall and sheds a tear. I know God loves all creatures; but, still, Nick has to be more important than the little sparrow right? Please wrap my boy in your comforting grasp God. Send the angels too because their wings are soft. Wrap them around Hallie too because she is hurting... Please God....

Nick's Mom

Monday, August 2, 2010 7:02 AM

I keep seeing two little brown-haired rascals running all over the two yards, mine and your parents', laughing, playing and having a good time. Right now laughing and running are beyond your reach, but I believe you will get back to enjoying your family and your life. Your strength will be an inspiration to many who might end up with such serious injuries and I hope you tell your story so that others can have hope and courage. You and your family are in my prayers. I'm wishing all the very best for you. Love, Marianne

Marianne Leake

Monday, August 2, 2010 9:01 AM

Nick, I have been reading a book, *God Never Blinks, 50 Lessons for Life's Little Detours*. I know you have a long tough battle ahead of you but know you can get through it if you keep the following in your mind:

You can get through anything life hands you if you stay put in the day you are in and don't jump ahead. The only day worth living is the day you are in. Each morning start from scratch & just try to live in today. Break the task, challenge or fear into bite size pieces. If 24 hours is too much to stay in, take it by the hour, moment by moment. It is not hard to live through a day, if you can live through a moment.[5]

---

5   God Never Blinks, Regina Brett, 2010 by Regina Brett, Grand Central Publishing, Hatchette Book Group, New York, New York.

I know your courage, strength and a lot of prayers will get you and Hallie through this. Dave, Kristen and I send our prayers.

Darlene Giffin

Monday, August 2, 2010 5:00 PM

Nick and Hallie, Your strength in this time of great challenge is truly inspirational. I am so glad to hear that one surgery is successfully behind you. Each hour, each day, will bring you a little closer to healing and returning home among those who love you so very much. I am proud of you and know that Grandma and Grandpa are looking down and keeping watch over you. I wish you did not have to endure this, but know you are blessed with courage, inner strength and the extraordinary support of your family. We love you!!! Your cousin Laura and girls

Laura Kulwicki

Monday, August 2, 2010 7:36 PM

Nick, once this hideous road of pain comes to an end and you are home on the mend again, you are going to realize what an inspiration you have been to all of us. We will look at our different crosses to bear in this life a little differently because of you. We can't wait for the day to give you a big hug that we might have taken for granted in the past. We love you soooo much!

Aunt Ceal and Uncle Vic

Monday, August 2, 2010 9:27 PM

Hi Nick, I just wanted to let you know when we got home last night the kids were asking how you were. Then when we said our prayers, both of them – unprompted prayed for you to feel better soon, so I am certain their wishes will come true. We love you, hang in there and be strong. Lori/Chris/The kids

Lori DiCola

From our Blog: Tuesday, August 3, 2010 11:39 AM, EDT

Quick update: surgery #2 down. The doc says his left arm burn was pretty much a mirror image of the right so he had practice from yesterday. He is on his way to recovery right now. More to follow later.

From our Blog: Tuesday, August 3, 2010 2:11 PM, EDT

IMPORTANT before I begin: Nursing staff has ordered a NO VISITORS except for immediate family. These surgeries are extremely grueling on Nick and they are compounding on each other. He needs to have the exposure to infection limited as well as his energy conserved to heal. We will post just as soon as he can have visitors again. Thank you for your understanding.

OK, day two surgery is now complete and as Hallie said it was a mirror image of day one. They grafted the complete arm, top of the hand and fingers too. Having had both hands and arms done, now they are both completely wrapped. It irritates him even in his hazy state. They will stay that way undisturbed for five days each to allow the grafts to "take". He is more confused today but he is also coming off of the effects of two consecutive days of anesthesia. He now also has two post-surgery sites, and two post-donor graft sites, which are located on both upper thighs and both sides of his chest. These are more painful than the burn sites because they have fresh nerve endings. Yikes! All in all, everything looks good. We are halfway through the required surgeries, and we think we are proceeding to surgery number 3 tomorrow. But there is a slight chance that there will be a break until Thursday. Not quite sure on that. We think surgery number 3 is Wednesday as planned.

I want to take this opportunity to say that this blog was initially started to help us get the word out to family and friends of Nick's condition. The fact that they in turn have posted messages to him was a nice bonus. What it has blossomed into is something beyond anything I could ever have imagined. It is a total outpouring of love, caring, faith, inspiration, neighbor-helping-neighbor, bonding and pure unbridled American spirit at its best. Thank You just isn't enough. I don't know the words to express what is in my heart. You are all the blessings we need right now.

I always knew that Nick was Hallie's rock. But I have learned that Hallie is also Nick's. Watching her during this last week, and especially these last two days has shown me that. When we are alone with Nick, especially in pre-op and post-op when he is at his worst, she speaks to him so lovingly. Ok she always does that. But today she was like steel, no tears. He was very anxious because he thought he had to get out of the bed because he had a job he had to print! Hallie was the one who softly convinced him that no, he did not have to go anywhere. He had just had surgery and he was to try to relax. Then later, he asked about The Bachelorette! I was the one who should have been able to be Hallie's rock, but at that moment, she filled that role.

The last few days here in the waiting room, seeing all the visitors who have come to see Nick has touched me more than I can say. He is a much-loved young man! Let's just say it's been a Love fest! All of his friends, I loved all of the hugs guys! And you gals too! Some of you I've known forever, some I just met, doesn't matter. You all love him. I come from a close family so I have especially felt the love from my immediate family: Skip, children, grandchildren, siblings and spouses, which of course includes my many nieces and nephews. My mother in law, who lives with us and can't come up to visit but is here in spirit every day, my father in law and his wife who is battling cancer. My kid's dad and his wife and kids, Ralph, sisters Deb and Dianne and Tim, etc also have been feeling all the same emotions. DeeAnn I have to tell you thank you for loving my baby all these years! I know you care!!! We've had some good talks these last couple of days!

Hallie's family, her dad, Tom, mom, Diana, Grandma, LuEllen, Aunt Pam, Uncle Mike and Cousin Teresa, who set up the donation website and many other aunts and uncles. My neighbors have been great, so have Nick and Hallie's neighbors - Nate, Matt, Nick and Aaron and everyone else on the scene, you will have my gratitude forever. My Premier Family, what can I say, you have totally wrapped me up, I feel your love! Cathy and TC, thanks for going over with Norma the night of the accident, you were so thoughtful to think of that! My special "card club" you mean the world to me, my girls! Thank you for holding me close. My Cruiser Friends, who I haven't seen in a long time, thank you, and I miss you. I also have to add, Nick so looks forward to reading the messages. He asks Hallie many times a day to read them to him. They encourage him more than you know..... We Love you ALL....

Nick's Mom

From our Blog: Tuesday, August 3, 2010 10:54 PM, EDT

(Hallie) I would just like to add to Nick's Mom's post. I am truly in awe of all the love and support that you all are showing to my wonderful husband, myself and family. It means so much to all of us! First and foremost we are so lucky to have so many people praying for Nick's recovery. This is the most important thing! Every Prayer helps!!! Also everyone offering to help out with things has really taken a huge burden off of my shoulders so that I can stay here with Nick. Maryanne, Dave, Dad, Marcy, Skip, Dave and DeeAnn, aunts, uncles, cousins, neighbors and all of our friends, you have all done so much! Also, we are so blessed that so many people are considering our future expenses! Thank you Teresa and Aunt Pam for organizing the Nick Fund, everyone who has made donations, offered to organize fundraisers, and trusts! I am also glad to see that people are coming together through all this. Two of our neighbors, Diane and Mrs. Wolfe stopped by today and gave us a collection from the entire neighborhood! In light of this awful situation, it is so nice to see the good in so many people. It is a breath of fresh air. We are so thankful for everything!!!

Hallie

Tuesday, August 3, 2010 12:20 AM

Nick & Hallie, Just a note to let you know I, along with friends, are praying for you...That the pain will not be outrageous, that you will continue to hang on day by day, or hour by hour, however you can cope the best, that complications will not set in, that you get the best of care, and that we will be able to see the good come out of this situation. From living next door, I am able to see that you have a strong base of encouragers and for that I am grateful. Hang in there. One thing the accident did do was draw the neighborhood together a bit more. I've actually met more neighbors because of this and there is definitely a drawing together and a positive concern for you, Hallie. I will do my best to keep your flowers from wilting ☺ Hang in there and just take life a day at a time. (Easily said...!) And "mom", keep your chin up. I am not a mom, but I am a pediatric home care nurse. I think

there are few things harder than watching a child of yours suffer.
Nick and Hallies' neighbor next door.

Sharon Mick

From our Blog: Wednesday, August 4, 2010 2:09 PM, EDT

He went into his third surgery at 2PM. They are doing the right leg and taking today and tomorrow's skin during today's operation. This is because they are taking it from his back and it will just be easier to get it all at once. More to follow later.

From our Blog: Wednesday, August 4, 2010 10:21 PM, EDT

Sorry this is so late everybody, it's been a long day. This has been Nick's most grueling day yet. He had his 3rd of 4 skin grafts, today to his right leg. They did the whole leg from just above the knee down including the top of the foot and the toes. They did an awful lot today. They harvested his entire back, using half of it for today, and the other half will be used for tomorrow's surgery on the other leg.

They also changed his central line, switching over to the other groin to avoid infection. A good thing. Another item was that they had to change his feeding tube type to one that goes lower into the small intestine. His stomach is much distended, very uncomfortable with edema, which means retaining fluids. This is caused from all of the anesthesia and medications from all of the surgeries. This different type of feeding tube is supposed to help with that. They tried to put it in before surgery in the room but it was too uncomfortable for him so they stopped and did it in OR. They took an X-ray before releasing him back to the room but once those results came in they found that the placement wasn't right and it had to be replaced. Since he now has a pain pump he was out of it and didn't realize what was going on, Thank God. So now the feeding tube is in the right place and he can get some nutrition and help the tummy too.

He has not even opened his eyes really since coming back down from surgery. We have not even been able to go into his room because his respiration has been so rapid. He is not in distress or anything, it is just a sign that the body has been through a lot, is in pain and needs to rest and recuperate....until tomorrow when we do it all over again. That's right; surgery #4 is tomorrow BUT IT IS THE LAST ONE!!! Keep praying everybody. Keep praying that everybody keeps up the strength and health and most especially and most importantly NICK KEEP UP THE STRENGTH, STAMINA, & HEALING HE NEEDS MORE THAN EVER!!!!

Nick's Mom

From our Blog: *Thursday, August 5, 2010 6:32 PM, EDT*

SURGERY IS OVER! Four surgeries in four days and Nick has completed them! Everything went really well, the doctor said he did great. I can't tell you the relief we all feel that this part is behind him. I am so grateful to God for continuing to see me, our families and all who care for all of us through this crisis. I am continuing to say the "Serenity Prayer" (Thank you Cherie for that tangible reminder too! She dropped off at the hospital a beautiful cross inscribed with The Serenity Prayer.) We are so glad that Nick was so diligent about working out, eating right and staying in such good shape. That is a huge plus that is helping him so much right now. Nick is resting quietly as I am writing this post. I keep looking up at him and feel comfort that his pain pump is delivering the medication to him and he is peaceful. You moms know what it is to see your child in pain and not be able to do anything to stop it. I think we all feel like a wet noodle about now.

So what's next? Well, the pain won't magically be over just because the surgeries are. He still has to heal from where the skin was harvested which remember was his entire back, his entire chest and his upper legs. We haven't been told how long to expect for these to heal but he does get daily dressing changes on these areas which he doesn't like. Tomorrow will be a day of rest for him other than the dressing change I just spoke of.

They have to actually take him out of his bed to do this. THIS by the way is a good thing because in his words this morning before surgery "This bed sucks". He ended up with a bed too small for him yesterday after surgery. Remember this is a children's hospital and somehow the bed that he got is a tad smaller than the others. He just fits on it. When they raise his head up it doesn't seem to fit him right. In Nick's lingo, let's just say, he's not a fan! He actually asked his doctor right before surgery for a new bed. Not a question he was used to getting I'm sure! Anyway, when they have him out of the bed tomorrow for the dressing change, they are doing a switch to a different bed.

Then the next big moment will be Saturday. That is the day when the dressings on the first graft site, the right arm come off. Then we see what to expect next.

I also want to mention that during all four of Nick's surgeries he has had to get a lot of blood. Even though it isn't possible at this point to donate blood directly to Nick, if you would like to donate blood to Akron Children's Hospital since so much was used that benefitted Nick, please consider doing so. Thank You!

If you are just checking the journal for the first time today, don't miss the post I made earlier in the day. You might get a little chuckle from it. However, my older son thinks I gave a little TMI at one point. Oh well, I'm a mom....

Love you all!!!

Nick's mom

From our Blog: Thursday, August 5, 2010 11:40 AM, EDT

The Canton Repository posted a beautiful story about the generosity of Nick and Hallie's neighbors. We are so blessed to be among so many people; family, friends, neighbors, and complete strangers who love and support Nick. He truly is an inspiration to us all! Nick's Sister, Marcy

Please see the link below for the complete story: http://www.cantonrep.com/newsnow/x1519716361/Lake-Twp-neighbors-donate-to-man-hurt-in-explosion

Here is the complete newspaper story:

Lake Twp. neighbors donate to man hurt in explosion
By Lori Monsewicz
CantonRep.com staff writer
Posted Aug 04, 2010 @ 02:25 PM
LAKE TWP.—

A Lake Township woman and her friend's 12-year-old daughter collected $600 from their small neighborhood within four hours.

It will go to a Greentown area neighbor who was badly burned in a boat explosion last week at his home.

Nick DeWalt was using a workshop vacuum to clean sawdust in his boat inside his garage on July 27 when gas fumes ignited and caused the boat's gas tank to explode.

He suffered burns to more than 46 percent of his body, according the family's internet blog. He remains in the Akron Children's Hospital's burn unit, where, a spokesman said Wednesday; his condition was listed as fair.

Neighbors Brenda Wolfe and Liz Serena heard of DeWalt's injuries and decided to help.

Wolfe and Serena's daughter, Diana Serena, began knocking on doors on four streets in their small neighborhood Sunday and Monday night. Liz Serena had to work and couldn't help them collect.

Wolfe and the Serena's gave the money to DeWalt's wife, Hallie DeWalt, on Tuesday night.

"We just felt bad and wanted to help him out a little bit," Diana Serena said. She said she checks his condition daily on the website.

"We know there are lots of expenses," Wolfe said.

She said that although the neighbors didn't discuss what the exact use of the money, people gave me anywhere between $2 and $110. Some gave $40, others $60 and $70, Wolfe said.

The neighbors had heard about the explosion.

"Everybody knew and they didn't bat an eye" at donating, Wolfe said.

Each contributor also signed a get-well card.

Hallie DeWalt noted the donation on the website: "In light of this awful situation, it is so nice to see the good in so many people—it is a breath of fresh air. We are so thankful for everything!!!"

The website also details his surgeries and skin grafts, described as "extremely grueling."

Copyright 2010 CantonRep.com. Some rights reserved [6]

Thursday, August 5, 2011 12:41 PM, EDT

Nick, Your positive attitude and sheer determination in the face of adversity is truly awe inspiring to me! It is said that the

---

6   The Repository, Lake Twp. neighbors donate to man hurt in explosion By Lori Monsewicz, CantonRep.com staff writer , Aug 4, 2010

mark of a person's true character is revealed not when things are good or easy but when faced with true hardship. You should feel proud that you have so many family and friends praying and rooting for you every minute of your ordeal. The way you carry yourself and treat others in your life with care and respect (hey – that's how you roll!) is what is going to propel you to a 100% recovery sooner than later. This spring I met Coach Viscounte, your D Coordinator at Lake. I mentioned that you were my cousin and he replied, without missing a beat, "Oh yeah, Nick. He had a big interception against Buchtel. Nick was one of the toughest hard-nose players I ever coached." I can't think of a better compliment!

Take care and take it easy on those nurses!!! Love, Chris & Lori

Chris DiCola

From our Blog: Friday, August 6, 2010 1:37 PM, EDT

I just thought I would do a quick update today so you would know what is going on. First let me start by saying thank you to Jen Wolf, an old high school classmate of Nick's. We got the following message from her today:

I went to high school with Nick and while I didn't know him well, I was so sad to hear of his accident and check the site all the time for updates. Sounds like he has a strong circle of people around him and that you are very loved! I just saw that he is a big Browns fan, and I am friends with Josh Cribbs. I will see him next Thursday so I was going to get a football signed to Nick if you think that would cheer him up. I was just wondering how to get it to his Mom, wife or a friend who could take it to him. Just let me know!

Jen Wolf (Cox)

WOW! Nick will be over the moon about this! Thank you soooo much!

Note: Josh Cribbs did indeed autograph a football for Nick. Check out the photo section for the picture of Nick receiving the ball. I read something recently that shows just what a big heart Josh Cribbs really has. His college alma mater, Kent State University, made it to the College World Series in baseball. Josh made sure that his school had plenty of cheering fans at the games by buying 53 tickets and chartering a bus to take the fans to Omaha, Nebraska. This was the school's first time at the World Series. What a guy!

This is a day of rest for Nick. They are keeping his pain pump running and even upped it a little so it stays ahead of the pain. The goal is to keep him comfortable. He opens his eyes from time to time to take a sip of Gatorade®, water and even asked for his favorite "Californian" that Skip introduced him to years ago, a mix of Seven UP® and Welch's® Grape Juice (Nick insists on Welch's® brand!)We brought the ingredients to the hospital to have them on hand. At this point Nick can have whatever he wants to drink. Since he can't press his pain pump himself we watch for signs of distress. It delivers medication automatically, but we are to press the button at least every 45 minutes. So we are watching him. Hawk-eyeing him.... It is so nice to see him resting comfortably...

I just read the messages and saw a one from someone who read Nick's story in the Repository. Her name is Connie. Her message touched me on many levels as have the other complete strangers who are posting that don't even know Nick are moved to post. But Connie noted that she too has online blog site so, Connie, I will add you to my prayers for what you have been going through as well. She noted that she ends her posts with the words With God All Things Are Possible. I want you to know that I have a sign on the desk in my home office that says, With God All Things Are Possible...

Nick's Mom

NOTE: There is more detail about all four days of surgery in my Personal Journal Entries to follow. You will see raw emotion oozing from the words, but I believe the daily chronicle is an important part of this journey...

From My Personal Journal: Friday, August 6, 2010

A week has gone by since I wrote here last, but I have poured my heart out in my daily posts on the blog. Right now I am sitting keeping vigil over Nick as he sleeps. This is his well-earned day of rest after four long, grueling days of surgeries. So today he rests... Last weekend is a blur in my mind right now. I remember each day began with waiting for the dreaded bath and skin peel then the re-dressing. We were so happy when they left his head unwrapped and we could see his face again! We felt like progress! When they removed his catheter and he peed by himself meaning the catheter didn't have to go back in, it was another small victory. I actually told two strangers that he peed! That prompted Marcy to call me Grandma DiCola! That was soooo something she would have done.

Monday was his first surgery day. They started with his right arm since it is his dominant one. They took the donor graft skin from his upper thighs and chest on the right side. It was one to one match. That means same size skin with no stretching. The only area that was two to one was behind the arm in the triceps area. Surgery took almost four hours and they had to do the top of his hands including his fingers. The skin is attached with metal staples. Think like paper staples except the ends aren't turned in, they are straight. They have a special tool to remove them. The graft is covered with dressings and an ace type bandage that is irrigated and wet down from time to time.

Tuesday was pretty much a mirror image of Monday's surgery only on the left arm. The skin was taken from left upper thigh, both front and back and upper chest. Same as the day before. Hallie and I stay with Nick in his room before surgery. By this time he is really thirsty having had all fluids cut off at midnight. They come for him and we follow the bed up to Pre-Op. There we wait with him where he mainly has his eyes closed. Then when the OR is ready for him, they come for him.

On the first day there was some confusion as to where they would put his identifying name badge since they had completely taken all his dressings off all limbs and had only sterile linens on him. They seemed stumped as he didn't have a catheter in yet. (Remember, YEA, he peed!) They were going to re-catheterize him in surgery. So I suggested they stick it around the feeding tube. They were like, ok, that's a good idea! And that is what they did. Nick didn't appear fond of that sticker right in front of his lips though as he kept giving it a pretty good puff of air from time to time. When he came out of surgery, it was gone.

While we were waiting, the hospital photographer showed up to photograph his "before" wounds. We were told it was a teaching hospital from the beginning and knew they would photograph his journey. But there was no way Hallie or I were going to permit this photographer from taking his pictures right then. Nick was completely unprotected and was covered with sterile linen. Not only would he be very cold if uncovered, but, the risk of infection was too great in that non-sterile environment. That photographer would have had to take both of us down to get to him. He eyed both of us then said he would take the photos in the OR. Damn straight.

When Day three of surgery dawned, Hallie and I were seriously dreading it. We hated everything about it. Leaving Nick, walking to Pre-Op, watching the doors close in the OR, the wait, all of it. I would wait to break down usually as he was wheeled out of my sight into the OR. There is something about seeing his head lying on that pillow fading from my view that just tears me up.

Day three proved to be the worst. Once the Doctor talked to us, and it was quite a while before he did, he said he had harvested his entire back to use for today's as well as tomorrow's surgery. They also were putting in a new central line in the opposite groin to reduce chance of infection. It seemed like forever after the Doctor talked to us and said we would be able to go back to Post Op in about 15 minutes.

After a long time, we started to go to the desk to check status, and we saw nobody was there. We thought, "Oh No, did we miss him?!" So I picked up the phone and got re-routed by mistake to NICU. (Neonatal Intensive Care Unit). After some frantic conversation on my part, I got directed to the PACU (Post Anesthesia Care Unit) and was told we would be able to come back in about 10 minutes, they were still working with him. They did, in fact, come out for us in about 10 minutes.

This was the worst day in the PACU. Nick's heart rate seemed so high along with his respiration, which was a direct result to his body's response to pain - three days in a row. When it was time, we did the well-known walk behind his bed and waited this time in the outer waiting room. But today ended up being different.

The nursing team said they didn't want a party in there. There were a lot of us in the waiting room. Finally at about almost 9 PM, they said we could come back. But not before we had the feeding tube thing. He had a puffy belly this morning, and it was really hard. They decided to try putting a different feeding tube in that went lower, into the top of

food go directly there and i

tried to do it in the room wi

to surgery. He begged her tc

of the room for this, thank (

had to do in the OR. A Gast

to be sure it was in the righ

they didn't want to release hi

correctly. The anesthesia pair

could go before x-ray results came in.

Later when a long time had gone by, Hallie suggested we eat some of their Anniversary cake that was in the kitchen refrigerator, so I went to go get it. I passed his room and saw three people in there sitting him up. I asked the girl taking me to the kitchen what they were doing to him. She said they had to check placement of x-ray since tube had been in his esophagus. I wanted to know when they replaced it.

She said it must have been done in the OR. I said that when we were in the PACU they hadn't gotten results yet so if she had them and the tube was in esophagus, it had to have been replaced in his room, NOT the OR. She had me speak to the charge nurse. This nurse kept trying to read the computer screen and seemed unable or unwilling to give me answers. She had the nursing supervisor come sit next to her and asked me to go sit in the waiting room and they would come soon and notify us. When she finally came in, she said the tube had gone into the esophagus but now was where it needed to be. She completely avoided my questions of earlier, and I didn't press it as Hallie was already at the breaking point. I'll explain in a minute. I still think they had to replace the tube in his room. I just hope he was out of it.

breaking point: We found out that a little boy
e burn unit has C-DIFF. When Hallie heard C-DIFF
was contagious she freaked out. She was sure she had
ause the little boy had been in the inner waiting room and
e had laid her head down and sort of sprawled on one of the tables so she just knew she had it. I mean she was really upset. It was like all the anxiety over Nick was coming out and nothing we could say would help. When she finally calmed down, it was the nurse talking about Nick's tube that did it. She never did get to go home today. Everyone didn't leave until about 10:30 PM. David and Marcy finally made me leave around 9:30 PM swearing they would text me as soon as the tube was in. I was near hysterics that he would be in pain; in spite of the fact that I knew it was necessary. I left and sobbed in the car as I drove. They texted a little after 10 PM to let me know the tube was in and he never woke up.

Thursday was surgery number four. The dread in my stomach was like a palpable thing. We never got the exact time for the surgery the night before but had figured since Wednesday's was at 2 PM; it would be 2 PM again. At 8 AM I was almost ready to leave except for getting my last minute things together when Hallie texted me that they had moved his surgery up to 10 AM. I freaked out. That meant they would be coming for him maybe before 9 AM. I knew I had to see him before he left his room so Hallie and I would walk with him to Pre-Op just like we did the previous three mornings. For some odd reason, I didn't want to change the order of things because I was afraid I would jinx it. I can't explain it. When I updated the journal for the day, I equated it with Nick's rituals on the Fridays of senior year of football season. Had to eat six soft-boiled eggs for breakfast, sit in the same chair, wear the same underwear, etc. For me, this was just like game day.

Nervously I had torn out of my driveway and down the street driving way too fast. I got to the hospital with very little time to spare before they took him. Hallie and I took the all too familiar walk up to Pre-Op. Once there, we found that there was a delay in surgery, and we ended up waiting in Pre-Op for I think close to 45 minutes. His good friend "Ned" (his name really is Ryan, but for some reason I've always called him Ned) was leaving that day for Atlanta to attend a wedding of their good friend, Todd. This was a wedding Nick and Hallie had planned on attending too. Anyway, Ned and his wife, Nikki were out in the surgery waiting room, and I'm sure he was devastated he'd missed seeing Nick since they'd moved up his surgery time, before he left town. Hallie, when hearing how long the delay was, went and got Ryan so he could see him. I'm glad he got to see him.

The time came for him to go into the OR. Once again we watched him get wheeled through the double doors. Nurse Betty, her compassion shining from her eyes, patted my shoulder. Again for the fourth day the tears fell. We made our way to the surgery waiting room and we waited... When we saw Dr. McCollum's handsome face, he had good news for us. All went well!

Now it was time to wait, five days to check his left leg graft progress, but only two days left to go before the site of the first graft could be checked – his right arm. We waited to be called back to the PACU, and this time he was back into a corner as there were a lot of kids in there today. I remembered prior to his first surgery Nick being warned that when he woke up in the PACU it would seem like he was in hell with all the kids screaming...after all, it was a children's hospital! Well, here we were. It seemed like they got him out of there in shorter order than before, as they were sensitive to the noise.

Before we knew it, we were making the walk down to his room. How glad we were that all four surgeries were behind us! Friday we took a breath and just laid low. Nick even had a day of relative rest with nobody really messing much with him.

Saturday was the first day of checking the graft site, the right arm. Dr. M wasn't in this weekend, so the information came from whomever we could talk to, nurses, those who attended, even two students who had been in the room who described the scene as "intense". Karrie, David's wife, is rotating through this hospital right now for nursing school, but didn't get to watch because of being a relative. But the report we got was that the grafts looked good and only a few staples came out on the shoulder.

Sunday was pretty much a repeat for the left arm. But HUGE news was Dr. M told Hallie she could come in and see. Then Dr. M said, "Mom, you too!" I'm glad I'd had no prep for this to get nervous and anxious. I just stilled myself and went in. But since I didn't know what to expect, they looked far better than what I think I expected. The worst part was his cringing as they gingerly removed the dressing from his leg. The Dr. said they looked "perfect, 100%". But Hallie told me I couldn't write the 100% part in the blog so as not to jinx it until they checked the other leg. But I can write that here in my journal!

So Tuesday they checked #4 and now it's unanimous...all grafts were a success and PRISTINE is the word that was used! They started physical therapy and the afternoon physical therapist said "Rumor has it that these are the best grafts they have ever seen!" WOW! The Dr. said all is up to Nick now. It's nutrition, physical therapy and his exercise. So Hallie is on the case getting him to eat! They also need him to do the breathing thing again, once an hour, ten times each when he is awake. I guess I'll nag on that one.

Friday, August 6, 2010 2:23 PM

Dear Maryanne, Skip, Nick & Hallie, It is always said that you can tell a lot about a person by the friends they have. You all are a bunch of loved people!! It is wonderful to read the messages posted here and to know how everyone is praying and thinking of Nick every moment! I know that will help him heal, and it has to help all of you as well!

I am so glad that Nick's surgeries are behind him now and he can begin to heal! Nothing but positive thoughts and a bright future ahead! I will continue to pray for a speedy recovery so Nick can be home in time for football season and the Brown's kickoff! Love, Adrienne

Adrienne Dawes

Friday, August 6, 2010 8:43 PM

Nick, my dear sweet son. If I could I would trade places with you in a second. You don't deserve this. You are kind, have a big heart and you are always there at a drop of a hat to help. I know how you take care of me. You and David do all my heavy stuff. I would be lost without you. I am so lucky to have the 3 kids I got. I know you can get through this. You set your mind to it and you accomplish it. You have never failed at anything. I can't wait till I get to see you. It's time to beat up David & Pigburg. Love, Skip.

Skip Shaw

Friday, August 6, 2010 10:49 PM

Hey Nick. I'm glad to hear the surgeries are behind you. I'm sorry; I just had to laugh when I heard the unfortunate state of affairs with that "Too small bed". In my mind I saw a small bed with your frame filling it from headboard to footboard. If I'd be an artist I'd draw you a caricature. But I understand, IT WAS

NOT FUNNY!!! Keep up the positive mindset. You may feel a bit mummified, but your determination will prevail! I continue to pray for you all.

I'm going to leave you with some verses that became very special to me in 2004 when our church building on Market Avenue burned down.

"For I know the plans I have for you," declared the Lord, "plans to prosper you and not to harm you, plans to give you a hope and a future. Then you will call upon me and come and pray to me, and I will listen to you. You will seek me and find me when you seek me with all your heart" Jeremiah 29:11-13[7]

I find peace in knowing that God knows, sees, and cares about everything His people on earth go through. I do not write commentaries, so I'll let you interpret that as or if you wish. Keep your chin up!

Sharon Mick

From our Blog: Saturday, August 7, 2010 12:19 PM, EDT

Today was the first "take-down" day. I'm learning terminology I never knew existed. "Take-down" is what they call taking off the dressings from the skin graft surgery to look at the area to see the progress of the grafts actually taking. I am happy to tell you that the entire right arm, which was the area of the first surgery, appears to be taking! Thank you God! They were wrapped after surgery in what they call a "wet" dressing because during the course of the last five days they had to irrigate them from time to time. Now they are wrapped in a "dry" dressing and will no longer have to be wet down.

Now I will give you a little more detail that is a little graphic although I think necessary so you understand just what Nick is

---

7   The Holy Bible: Jeremiah 29:11-13

enduring. Grafts are put into place with metal staples, lots of them. Think of the staples that come out of a paper stapler, only these have straight edges, not ones that turn in on the end. Just a few of the staples were removed today. Not pleasant. As a result of that, the dressing change and the treatment to his donor graft area an incredible amount of pain medication needed to be given to him to reduce his pain. He is doing well, but as I sit here writing this post he is sleeping. We have been told to expect that during this next week each day will bring more of the same. This is an incredibly painful process and the main goal of his nursing staff is to keep him as comfortable as possible. For now that is going to mean a lot of medication. The nature of burns is they hurt more at the beginning, they hurt less as they heal. That also goes for the donor graft areas.

I have to say a special thank you to Jan Nutter, from the Premier Designs Prayer Ministry. She has been sending many prayers heavenward on Nick's behalf since the very beginning. Not many companies have a prayer ministry service as part of their corporation! But Premier does, and I am thankful.

I am excited that Hallies' Aunt Pam and Uncle Mike are in town this weekend from PA. She is the one who set up the website donation link. Pam is Hallie's dad, Tom's, sister. I can't wait to give them a big hug!!! It will be good for Hallie to see them. Her dad has been a huge source of support for Hallie too. It was also nice that Hallie's mom, Diana, made the trip in from Philadelphia yesterday. Hallie knows how much she cares. I also spoke with her grandma, LuEllen, and that whole side of the family loves Nick and Hallie to distraction too. They have a large network of love surrounding them.

I have just been informed that Nick & Hallie's neighbor, Fran Hamric and Nick's aunt, Ceal DiCola have set up a Burn Victim Fund for Nick DeWalt at the bank. Fran and Ceal also made signs and donation cans and placed them at various locations throughout the area. I was completely bowled over when Ceal told me about this. There is so much good in so many people!

Nick's Mom

Saturday, August 7, 2010 6:04 AM

Dear Nick and Hallie, Just wanted to remind you that we are still praying for you daily...living across the street provides all of us with daily nudges to keep praying and rejoicing each day that you are recovering from this accident...Hallie, if you all need meals or anything for at the hospital, please let us know...It has become an actual joy to read the many posts and journal entries as it allows everyone who cares to feel like we are a small part of your journey...thanks to your family for their diligence...writing is great therapy... In God's precious love,

Sonia Lavy

Saturday, August 7, 2010 10:07 AM

Dear Maryanne and Family, I pray for Nick continually. I have gone to a shrine in our area known for miracles and asked Padre Pio to heal him. I just want you to know you have many angels praying for you all. Much love, Ami

Ami Babgy-DiPietro

Saturday, August 7, 2010 12:45 PM

Hello Nicholas, You are constantly in our prayers daily. We are also praying for strength for Hallie and all your family especially your loving mom and my sister-in-law, Maryanne. You know she would go to the ends of the earth for her children or any member in her family. I have witnessed this many times over the years. She is the matriarch of our family! All our love, Aunt Ceal & Uncle Vic

Ceal DiCola

From our Blog: Sunday, August 8, 2010 1:37 PM, EDT

I am sitting here looking at my beautiful boy! His face is healing wonderfully which is a joy to see, let me tell you. Also they did the second "take down" on his left arm this morning and this graft is looking good too! I am so thankful! It was about a three hour process in all for them to unwrap both arms, remove some of the staples, redress, plus unwrap and redress his donor graft areas. They used a different type of wrap on his donor graft areas today so they may not have to mess with them daily, which I'm sure he will be very happy about. Tomorrow they will have a look at the right leg. He has been running a bit of a fever so they did some cultures, but no word on those yet.

He was more alert with Hallie for a bit last night and asked her a few questions. When I came in after they were finished with his dressings, he had his eyes open for a couple of minutes and told me he saw his arm. His voice is very soft and he has very little energy. He sleeps mostly all day. His Morphine® is delivered by pain pump and we are still instructed to push the button for him at least every 45 minutes to keep him comfortable on top of what is delivered automatically. Hallie told me that he was able to move his fingers of his right hand this morning and even pushed his button once!

They had told Nick that a couple of times a day to do some mild flexing to those fingers. Hallie has already seen him doing it. That just made the tears come to my eyes. That's the Nick we all know and love...the Nick who will buckle down and do whatever he has to do to meet this head on. He will persevere no matter what the pain. I know it. That's my boy. And Hallie will be right there beside him. And not just because she took that vow, "For better or for worse". She will be there because she loves him. Right now it is a little of the "For worse" part, but together for Hallie and Nick, there will be a whole lot of "For Better" to come. I know it....

Nick's Mom

Sunday, August 8, 2010 5:26 PM

Hi Nick, It made my heart smile when you lifted your bandaged fingers and waved goodbye to me this afternoon. Keep hanging in there. Eventually inch by inch will turn into mile by mile. We love you. Love, Karrie

Karrie DeWalt

Sunday, August 8, 2010 7:26 PM

Dear Nick, We were so saddened to hear about your accident. Your progress in recovery, though only one small step at a time, will bring hope that you will soon be back at home.

I always remember you helping your mom and Skip by coming over often with your lawn equipment on a trailer, and cutting the grass in their yard; as I drove by, as busy as you were, you always waved to me and gave a friendly smile.

I remember you walking your dog, Clipper, down the road.

I remember you waiting for the middle school/high school bus with Greg, Chris, and Craig...you were all just a little too young yet to drive to school, so you all had to endure that school bus just one more year!

I remember how proud your mom was when you played high school football; and she showed me your beautiful wedding photo.

I have been thinking of the right words to help you during this time of your healing, and I happened to drive by a church in Stow and the message board by the road read: "CLOTHE YOURSELF IN COMPASSION, KINDNESS, AND PATIENCE", I will borrow their message and pass it on to you, and your family and friends. We are all praying for your recovery. Love, Jeanette

Jeanette Mueller

Monday, August 9, 2010 6:22 AM

Nick, I received the following prayer in an email and immediately thought of you, Hallie and your mom: "Help me to start this day with a new attitude and plenty of gratitude. Let me make the best of each and every day to clear my mind so that I can hear from you. Please broaden my mind that I can accept all things. Let me not whine and whimper over things I have no control over. And give me the best response when I'm pushed beyond my limits. I know when I can't pray, you listen to my heart. Continue to use me that I may be a blessing to others. Keep me strong that I may help the weak...keep me uplifted that I may have words of encouragement for others. There is no problem, circumstance, or situation greater than God. Every battle is in your hands for you to fight."[8]

Our priest said that in order to have a relationship with God that you have to spend time with him. I know these past few days a lot of people have increased their time talking to God because of you. I'm just so sorry you have had to endure so much pain to make this happen. We will continue talking to God on your behalf. We love you.

Darlene Giffin

---

8   Prayer, Author Unknown. http://d21c.com/moonbud/prayer.html

Monday, August 9, 2010 9:40 PM

Dear Nick – This evening I had the blessing of talking to your mom when she stopped by your home. As a mom of two sons also – I know her heart for you! I appreciated sharing time with her and watching her tears, as she said how proud she is of you...no one can relate to a mother more than another mom! Please continue to know we are thinking of you, Hallie and everyone. Can't wait to have you back home one day! Your home holds many memories for all of us who grew up with the Hirschman's and I pray it will be a haven for you and Hallie. Lovingly,

Sonia Lavy

From our Blog: Tuesday, August 10, 2010 1:50 PM, EDT

We are very happy to tell all of you that all four of Nick's skin graft surgeries were successful. To quote Nick's doctor, the word was "pristine"! He will continue to have them checked and dressed daily. In addition, he has started physical therapy. The PT will increase once they get him out of bed which we think will be in a couple of days. We realize that this is a slow process, and to tell you the truth we are not sure what all the steps are. They do keep him busy though. While it is exhausting for him, it is a necessary part of his recovery and he knows that. Sometimes he is more alert and he'll ask some questions or ask us to read to him from this site. He loves hearing the posts! Then in a few minutes, he falls back to sleep. At other times, he doesn't say much. When we are here, we take our lead from him so he can conserve his energy. If he is too tired from talking, he will be too tired to eat. But I know both he and Hallie have been able to spend some quality time in the evening when all is quiet and he is awake.

All in all we are happy and grateful with progress thus far. Stay tuned for further postings. Thank you all so much for your loving support!

Nick's Mom

From my Personal Journal: Wednesday, August 11, 2010

For the first time since the accident, I went to my office this morning. I had to do some database work, and then I went to Nick's office. Got here about 1 PM. He was getting his dressing changed and didn't get done until about 2:30 PM or so. When I saw him, he was sitting in a recliner and his face looks so good! He ate a good lunch! They are lowering his tube feeds during the day, hoping to increase his appetite. He had physical therapy right after lunch, which wiped him out. They then put him to bed, and he's been sleeping since about 5 PM. It's 6:10 PM now. He's still on the pain pump and getting less additional "pushes". He does get them before his PT's and dressing changes though. Can't wait for him to lose that catheter! They are sitting him up, and soon he'll be standing. One step at a time...

From our Blog: Thursday, August 12, 2010 12:46 PM, EDT

Hello to our loving, supporting family and friends...To say that you are amazing is such an understatement. I love words, I read words, I even make my living writing words, and yet, I just can't find the words to express what this total outpouring means to all of us. Fundraisers are in the works to help Nick and Hallie out. Donations have been coming in by way of cash and services. Food has been delivered. Offers of help have been more than I can list. Cards, messages, texts, each and every one is read by us and to Nick....and he savors each word. My nephew, Rick, even looked into donating his own skin when he heard that four grafts were needed. Although that wasn't possible, I was awestruck at his total willingness. Although it is not nearly enough, thank you to everyone from the bottom of our hearts.

Nick is progressing very well. His skin grafts including the donor graft areas continue to heal with no signs of infection. I keep hearing the words thrown around "best grafts they've ever seen". Wow, what a blessing! I'm sure his state of health and fitness had a lot to do with that.

His days continue to be action packed between dressing changes, occupational therapy, physical therapy and flex exercises that he does on his own in his bed to keep his wrists, fingers, hands, feet and ankles from stiffening up. Today is going to be a big day for him as they are going to stand him up on the floor for several seconds. This is a milestone! (**NOTE**: I just HAD to come in and edit this post with this paragraph...Nick not only stood, he took the few steps to his chair with the assistance of a walker and the nurse and therapist at his side of course. Now I'm crying again, but they're tears of joy!!!)

They have also reduced the amount of food he receives through his feeding tube in order to increase his appetite so he starts to take more food in the natural way. Hallie thought maybe I could make him my "potatoes" that he loves so much to sort of jump start his appetite. This was before they lowered his feeding tube amount. When Hallie suggested it to me, I couldn't wait to go to the store and buy the supplies. I left the hospital that night and did just that. The following morning I made a single batch of potatoes before coming up to the hospital.

My dilemma was, how much do I take up to the hospital? For those of you that know me, you know that I have a problem with food quantity. I always make lots of food! When I have my family over to dinner and everyone is done eating, they always joke that everyone could eat all over again with all the food that is left. Go ahead, make fun. But I have also been told by each of my children that they know when they come to dinner at my house that they never have to worry about the portion of food that they take on their plate or if there is enough to go around. They know they get care packages, and they know they will fill their bellies. I make sure of that. To me, that was the ultimate compliment.

They also know that they could bring someone with them at the last minute and there is enough food to feed them. Especially on Thanksgiving. I always loved to have a full table at Thanksgiving. The idea of having someone at my table who didn't have a place to go, whose family was far away, whatever the reason, those were the best Thanksgivings!

Now I've gone off on a tangent, haven't I! Back to the potatoes...Reluctantly I filled a small container and brought that to the hospital. It sure didn't look like enough to me, but Hallie told me several times only to bring a LITTLE. See she knows me. Nick enjoyed the very little bit he ate. Hallie helped him out!

Nick still has his pain pump as all of this therapy is painful, but he is doing extremely well and remains upbeat, positive with that determined attitude we all know and love about him.

The breathing machine is back! Once an hour, ten times when he is awake. I usually just set it on his tray table when it is time without saying anything. He just gives me that "look".

For now, we still have to keep the visitor policy restricted. He just has to use so much energy for all his therapy and it does exhaust him. We want him to heal as fast as possible so he can get home to Hallie! When he does get to have visitors we will ask that you keep your stay to no more than 10 minutes please. And if you have any sign of a cold, cough etc. STAY AWAY! Thanks for your understanding. Blessings to All!

Nick's Mom

Thursday, August 12, 2010 2:26 PM

Hey Nick, Hallie & AMA — Thanks so much for your beautiful and informative journal entries! And Hallie, I got your very sweet vm, so kind of you to find the time to get in touch!

I wanted to tell you all something. One of my oldest and dearest girlfriends is a nurse at Children's, but not in the burn unit. She of course has friends that do work in that unit. She has told me that the nurses all love Nick. They highly praise him and Hallie and AMA for being such kind and wonderful people! No big surprise there, just nice to know how well thought of you all are, even in light of the crisis you are living. It reminds me of: Live Simply, Love Generously, Care Deeply, Speak Kindly, And, Leave the Rest to God. [9]

Also in my office at home I have posted directly in front of me so I see it daily is: If God brings you to it, He will see you through it. Happy moments praise God, Difficult moments seek God, Quiet moments worship God, Painful moments trust God, Every moment thank God. [10]

Love that, and all of you.

More to come, as we are finalizing our pasta dinner fundraiser for Sunday, Oct. 3rd. I have everything at the printer and it will all be available for circulation soon. Also will

---

9   Live Simply Quote, Ronald Reagan. http://www.goodreads.com/quotes/show/128645

10   If God Brings You To It, Author Unknown. http://www.holybible.com/resources/poems/ps.php?sid=593

have wristbands and necklaces for sale as well, both are in production!! Much love, Cherie

Cherie Grescovich

From our Blog: Friday, August 13, 2010 11:36 AM, EDT

BIG NEWS!!! Nick walked in the hall! We are sooooo excited! He went out of his room and around the corner to the end of the short hall with his walker with the therapist by his side. Then they had him sit back in his recliner and they wheeled him back to his room! HUGE MILESTONE! Another BIG step onward is they are removing him from constant medicine from his pain pump. He will still be hooked up to it with the ability to push the button if he needs it, but he will be given meds by mouth regularly. He is resting now in preparation for his dressing change to be followed by his second PT this afternoon. We remain grateful to God for keeping his loving arms enfolded around our Nick throughout this journey.

Nick's Mom

From our Blog: Saturday, August 14, 2010 2:17 PM, EDT

I'm sure you have heard of the children's book *The Little Engine That Could* by Watty Piper. I used to read a bedtime story to my children every night and this one was a favorite for my kids, especially Nick. I always put a lot of animation into the story and into the voice of the little blue engine as he said "I think I can, I think I can, I think I can" as he made his way up the hill. In lots of ways I have thought about that story, *The Little Engine that Could*, these last couple of days. For instance: On Thursday, the goal of the therapist was to get Nick to stand bedside for about 30 seconds. In Nick's words, "If I'm standing, I'm walking"...and he took his first steps to his bedside chair.

On Friday, the therapist's goal was for him to take a short walk to the nurse's station. Again, Nick set his sights higher and he walked down and around the corner. When it was time for his dressing change and they wanted him to walk to the tub room door, his second walk of the day, he was visibly worn out. But not one to turn down a challenge, I saw him put on his "game face". And take that second walk he did! We stood and watched him do it, me with tears streaming down my face. But these were different tears, they were tears of joy! Now, today he raised the bar still higher. He walked a complete lap around the unit! Then he walked to the tub room, and got in the tub himself. I was here and watched him walk back. With each step, another accomplishment. I can almost hear him saying..."I thought I could, I thought I could, I thought I could!"[11]

Nick's Mom

From our Blog: Sunday, August 15, 2010 2:08 PM, EDT

Another good day everybody! Since it is the weekend, no physical therapy today. Some would consider this a day off...but Nick didn't take the day off. He wanted to get some exercise so he hit the hallway for some walking. Hallie, her dad, Tom, and I accompanied him on FOUR laps! What a guy!

More news...He still gets his daily baths and dressing changes but...they have started to unwrap his grafts as they heal. More progress! AND they have disconnected him from the pain pump, and he is totally on pills. Onward!!!

I will be able to update you all on yesterday's bake sale in a couple of days as soon as I get all the details. I also want to thank

---

11   The Little Engine That Could, by Watty Piper, 1976 copyright by Platt & Munk, an imprint of Grosset & Dunlap, a division of Penguin Young Readers, New York, New York

Darlene Giffin who stayed the entire time to help Joni and Ashley. Thanks so much to all of you!

One more quick thing...Skip was finally able to come up to the hospital today. He had a staph infection on his leg and was banned from seeing Nick. He was so happy to be able to see him! And Nick was happy to see him too!

Today's word for the day I would say is MOTIVATION!!! Love to All,

Nick's Mom

Sunday, August 15, 2010 4:40 AM

Maryanne, I have you in my heart always. I am so happy for you and Nick that he is recovering and all seems to be going extremely well. His angels abound. I continue to pray for him and you. I just had to tell you my very, very favorite childhood book was the Little Engine that Could. You made me realize how important reading to the little ones can be. I am going to make an effort to read to Valerie at night so she will have a favorite childhood book also. God Bless You all! Much love, Ami

Ami Bagby-DiPietro

Monday, August 16, 2010 8:01 PM

Hi Nick, This is from sappy Aunt Ceal. I just got back from visiting you and I can say I have witnessed a true miracle! You were sleeping, but the first thing I said as my jaw dropped open, "there is that beautiful face that I remember" before this whole scenario began. I should have said handsome face! All those prayers offered up for you and your sheer determination to get well is making me an even stronger believer in the power of God. When you did wake up, I told you that you looked 100% better than the last time I saw you! The progress that you are making,

I think will be entered in a few journals at the hospital! Keep up the good work and we will see you at home! Love you very much

Aunt Ceal & Uncle Vic

From our Blog: Tuesday, August 17, 2010 10:56 AM, EDT

Three weeks. When you are on vacation, three weeks passes in the blink of an eye. But I'm sure you all know that these past three weeks has seemed like an eternity. We've come a long way in these three weeks. Nick faced the biggest adversity he's ever faced in his life. And he faced it head on without batting an eye. All of us, his ever-widening support group included have been walking this road beside him, shedding tears for the pain he endured and pumping our fists in victory for each step forward he made. Well dear friends, I am happy to tell you that today, three weeks to the day after his horrific accident, our Nick has improved so much that HE IS BEING RELEASED FROM THE HOSPITAL!!!! Yes, he is going home to Hallie this very day! Krystal Lovette is at their home this very minute doing some last minute preparations and tonight Nick and Hallie will be enjoying some quiet time together.

We all know that God had his hand on Nick...to save his live, to send his angel, to give him presence of mind to act quickly and to preserve his face, to place the people there who were needed to act. We also know how very blessed we are to have so, so many of you sending your prayers heavenward on Nick's behalf. And for Hallie too. His hospital stay is ending, but his healing journey will continue for many months. Please continue your prayers. From the bottom of my heart I thank you. Love to all of you on this wonderful, wonderful day!

Nick's Mom

Tuesday, August 17, 2010 6:25 AM

Hey Nick, I cannot put into words how it felt to watch you walk down the hallway last night. There are not too many people who are strong enough mentally and physically to do what you are doing. I knew you were very tired last night when you went for the walk, but you know what you have to do to get home and you are doing it. The progress you are making is unbelievable! I showed the girls the picture of you sitting in your chair and their faces lit up! They can't wait to see you. Can't wait to have you back home! Dave

David DeWalt

From our Blog: Wednesday, August 18, 2010 7:44 AM, EDT

Good Morning Everyone! As I look out my window as I write this, I am surprised that I can still be amazed...but I can! Did you see how may visits there have been to this blog? OVER 5200! 5241 as of right now to be exact. I loved reading all the messages, and I'll bet Nick has already had Hallie read them to him. He loves them, so keep them coming. I want you to know that these updates are not going to stop with his homecoming. Nick still has a journey ahead of him. While the posts may not be daily, you will still be hearing from me....

Nick's Mom

From our Blog: Friday, August 20, 2010 10:04 AM, EDT

I have really been emotional these last few days! I can't really explain it, Nick is home, he is doing great, we are all very happy that he has started the recovery process. Hallie has been a rock! The last few days have been a little hectic, but it's all good! Nick is very diligent about doing all of the physical therapy exercises that he was sent home with, but then are you surprised? He is at the hospital right now for his first outpatient PT appointment.

He is wearing temporary compression bandages until he gets his permanent ones. He's being fitted for those today. I'm sure they are very warm. They have ceiling fans and lots of other fans going in their house but still he sweats. He has to wear this compression suit for one year. For this reason David and Karrie, Marcy, good friends, Ryan and Lisa Stewart and Skip and I are installing central air conditioning in their home. In fact, they are here right now. Many thanks to Greg from Accurate Air Flow Heating & Cooling for his generosity in helping us get this done for Nick & Hallie.

Shortly before the air conditioning guys got here, the team arrived to knock down the garage. Now, those of you that know me know that I can be a worry wart at times. My kids word it a little stronger and say I tend to freak out! So when the air guys and the garage guys were both here together, and the air guys thought they might not be able to get the air completely in today with the garage guys here, and Brody was barking like crazy, I was running around shutting all the windows so dust wouldn't get in the house, worrying that Nick would get home any minute and how was he going to stand the heat? Walk through with the debris in the air? Let's just say...Let the Freak-Out Begin! It took Marcy, David and Skip to talk me down!

About an hour and a half has passed now, and the air guys finished their job in the basement and just asked the garage guys to hold up a second so they could do what they had to do outside. So the end result will be....Nick will be cool today when he returns from his therapy appointment. I think my blood pressure might be back to normal by now.... Yes, it's all good!

Nick's Mom

From our Blog: Sunday, August 22, 2010 10:00 AM, EDT

Everyone has been soooo wonderful. People have been stopping over at Nick and Hallie's house to drop off needed supplies, things we have needed, things we didn't even know we needed, food, ice, health care items, thank you all so much.

As you know, Nick went to his first PT appointment on Friday. There they got new instructions for the dressing changes for his back. While it continues to heal, it is a slow process. They would like him to stay off of his back for half of the day, but that is pretty hard to do. The daily bath and dressing change is about a two hour process. He's usually ready for a good rest afterwards. The time that this takes place varies, and I help for part of this new process. Hallie is wonderful. I got my first lesson yesterday.

On Friday afternoon, the hospital had given Hallie a prescription for sterile bandaged rolls for his back that are medicated. Of course when I went to fill it, they had to be ordered and nobody had any. The pharmacist even helped call many local pharmacies. She finally found one that stocked it, but upon arrival, instead of being a roll it was an individual patch. I bought several. On Saturday in the midst of the dressing changing process we realized just how small these patches were and knew we didn't have enough. Luckily, Nick's good friend, Jesse Miller, had just arrived (hot water tank fix - another story!) and we sent him off to buy out the pharmacy of the little patches. I could literally write a long lengthy account of the many, many phone calls that took place to get ordered the rolls of medicated bandages needed for Monday, not to mention the supplies for Sunday's dressing change, but I'm already going to catch heck for going into this much detail... Suffice to say, never a dull moment!

Nick's Mom

From our Blog: Wednesday, August 25, 2010 8:50 AM, EDT

Good Morning Everyone Now that Nick is home from the hospital, his days have been occupied with his PT exercises, eating his required protein-enriched meals, taking walks around the living room, dining room and kitchen area of their home and of course the daily dressing changes. In between he has napped and enjoyed some visits. His spirits are good and he is talking about looking forward to getting to take a walk outside and the day he will be able to jog! That's my baby!!!

I'm sure you remember my post from last weekend about the patches and the rolls. On Monday, the rolls came in along with an extra jar of the cream that is needed to be applied on top. The only pharmacy that had them was Davies on West Tuscarawas Street in Canton. On Monday morning I asked DeeAnn, Nick's step-mom, if she could go out and pick them up and meet us at the house, which she was happy to do. The downside was that it turned out that Davies was a non-network provider. Yikes!

Hallie is a champion now at applying these dressings. I am happy to report that I see improvement every day to the areas of the donor grafts. These are very slow to heal though so we know it's not a quick process.

I am going to ask a favor...Keep Posting your Messages!!! Nick finds it so encouraging to read your posts. Although he is home now, and there isn't as much new information as there was when he was in the hospital, he needs to feel the love as much now - if not more than ever. We are all so lucky to have all of you, I mean that every fiber of my being.

God has a plan for each of us, I know that with all my heart. Somewhere, somehow all that's happened fits perfectly into that plan.

Nick's Mom

From our Blog: Friday, August 27, 2010 6:53 AM, EDT

Good Morning,

Well....Nick has been enjoying the sunshine! He has been taking a walk outside, just as he said he wanted to! His smile was worth everything when I saw him, he was just so happy to be out there. He stays out of the direct sun, and the last couple of days weather-wise have been perfect.

If you're not sick of yet another dressing story, I'll tell you one last quick one...we ran out of the large bandage that is used to cover his chest and back. Long story short, I couldn't find them ANYWHERE so had to buy rolls of the stretch gauze and wrap him up mummy style yesterday. Since you already know about the problem I have judging quantities of food, I didn't know how many rolls of gauze to buy. I was afraid, what if I don't buy enough and we run out mid wrap? So I bought 17 rolls! Yes we had enough, and yes we had some left over! Boy did we!

New appointment with PT today! AND WATCH THIS SPACE FOR A SURPRISE ANNOUNCEMENT!

Nick's Mom

From our Blog: Saturday, August 28, 2010 2:28 PM, EDT

I would like to thank you all for all the thoughts and prayers you have sent my way. I really enjoyed hearing and reading them. They helped lift my spirits everyday in the hospital. I am truly amazed by all the support. I am doing well and getting stronger by the day. I keep to my PT workouts and am walking up and down the street. I am working hard to get my strength back to get back to my normal routine. Again, thank you all for the thoughts and prayers!!

Nick

From our Blog: Tuesday, August 31, 2010 7:29 PM, EDT

Soooo did you all like the surprise? It was Nick making a post the other day! I held off posting because I wanted his words staying front and center! I'm sure he will continue to stay connected. He is doing so well. I swear he is the doctor and the Burn Unit's poster boy! They say if it wasn't for his level of fitness and nutrition regimen before the accident, he wouldn't have gotten out of the hospital when he did because his grafts wouldn't have healed so well so quickly! It sure makes us want to put our nose to the grindstone to eat healthy and workout doesn't it! Nick knows that he has his work cut out for him to get his agility back and he is up for the task! I am so proud of my boy!

I have to tell you something exciting that happened on Friday. I have been bursting to post about it. On Friday morning, a friend of mine, Monica Witmer, was driving through Hartville and saw a truck that said DeWalt-Guaranteed Tough. She came into the office and immediately told me about what she saw. She was all excited because she immediately thought of Nick! Well I was excited too. We both knew that it stood for DeWalt Tools. So I got online and soon found out that DeWalt Tools was doing a Guaranteed Tough nationwide tour that just so happened to be at Hartville Hardware THAT DAY starting in about fifteen minutes! So guess what I did? You betcha! I jumped in my car and drove up there!

Right there in front of Hartville Hardware was this big 'ole semi truck and another large stand, both emblazoned with the slogan DeWalt - Guaranteed Tough. I was BESIDE MYSELF!!! I parked right in front of the stand where three men were standing watching me practically run up to them. I had a flyer with me that had Nick's picture on it that told his story. I asked for a banner to use at our fundraisers and anything else DeWalt Tools could give us because Nick definitely lived out every letter, every word, of their slogan, Guaranteed Tough. The guys were very nice and agreed to indeed, send something on to Nick direct to his home. I couldn't resist adding that he would use DeWalt Tools for life! Now let's see what they send.

Later when I told Nick about it, he reminded me that when he was in high school I had scoured the country to purchase "DeWalt" bar stools for both him and his brother, David. I had also bought him a t-shirt that says DeWalt - Guaranteed Tough. In fact, he had it on yesterday when I stopped over. I had remembered about the stools but forgotten about the shirt and the slogan. It's just that the slogan means SO MUCH now. I might have forgotten it before, but I'll never forget it now.

Nick's mom

Note: A couple of months later a small banner did arrive direct from DeWalt Tools. Too late for the fundraiser, but it is proudly displayed along the wall of Nick's new garage.

From our Blog: Monday, September 6, 2010 10:59 AM, EDT

I hope all of you are enjoying this long holiday weekend. I love this weather! Nick continues to push himself to "check" off the goals on his list! On Thursday he asked me to drive him to his office. In his words, he wanted to "sniff around" a little. Although we didn't stay more than an hour, he was able to see firsthand that his shop was neat, (thanks to Cora, the dynamo!) the work was up-to-date and he was even able to sit at his desk and go through his computer a little bit. A couple of surprises were that he had two messages from potential new clients for job quotes! So that was exciting for him.

I have had many, many of you offer to come with me to Nick's office to volunteer their services in keeping his business up and running. Believe me, I have all of your names, and I may still call you! It's going to be a while before Nick himself can handle the day-to-day operations on his own again. There are some thank-you's in order... Right at the beginning, Nick specifically requested that I call Dean and Cora Frederick and ask them to take care of the day-to-day operations. (They had done the job before.) What he didn't know was they had already called me and volunteered! What Nick asked was that they keep track of their hours so he could pay them later. From day one, they made it clear that they were volunteering their time! I have known Cora and Dean for many years through the Buckeye Cruisers. We have shared many laughs around a campfire, (though we haven't been able to do that for far, far too long!) They are among the hardest workers and have the biggest hearts of anyone I know. I can't thank you enough! Others who have helped at Nick's business (called Advanced Fulfillment Solutions LLC) are Linda Byers (another Buckeye Cruiser), Ellen Cooper (Nick's cousin), Marcy DeWalt (sister), Jimmy DiCola (Nick's cousin)- who is a die-hard Steelers fan & has promised to don a BROWN's jersey in Nick's honor!!!) and Vic and Ceal DiCola (uncle and aunt). We love and appreciate you all!!!

We all know that Nick is surpassing all of the PT and OT expectations. Nick himself wants to get back to his fitness regimen. He wants to jog again. I'm sure his neighbors will see him doing just that. As a mom it makes me nervous. If I could, I would be running in front of him with a broom sweeping all loose pebble and twigs out of his path. (Think of the Olympic sport, curling!) Now, there's a picture for you!

Another goal for Nick is to drive. He is allowed to do that but was told to start slowly. I know he can't wait to be able to go to his office on his own, sit at his desk and take the reins back from me. I will be only too happy to turn them over. Nick, I hope you don't have to spend too much time going over and "fixing" the invoicing I did for you! In the meantime, it is a joy watching you progress.

One final thought...I said this to many people, almost from the beginning, and I will share it again with all of you now. I have always believed that things happen in life for a reason, and God has a plan for our lives. Sometimes the event changes the course of your life. Sometimes the way you respond to the event inspires others for a lifetime. I think both of those statements apply here. The thing that I said to several people starting with the early days in the hospital was that perhaps the reason for Nick having to endure all of this could have been to prepare him for his life's purpose. I believe that Nick could be a motivational speaker. I can see it clearly. As each day passes, I feel it stronger. I believe it.

Nick's mom

From our Blog: Tuesday, September 7, 2010 12:57 PM, EDT

Hello everyone, it's Nick again. Just wanted to update you on my status. I was cleared to drive on Friday and drove myself to work today. I also was out and got some new running shoes. I strapped them on yesterday and began a long walk. I started power walking for a while then I decided to walk a hill by my house. I felt so good I began to jog the hill and made it to the top. I walked a little more, and then jogged past about 3 or 4 more houses until I was home. I figured if I am walking fast, I can jog a little. It felt good, I was out of breath but boy did I feel like I accomplished something. Thanks again for all your prayers; they are giving me the power to get stronger every day.

Nick

From our Blog: Monday, September 12, 2010 10:59 AM, EDT

We have all been a witness to Nick's great strength and determination throughout his ordeal. We have seen him stand up to each and every challenge. As he moves into the next stage of his recovery process, the improvements won't be as visible to us...but they are vital for Nick. As his body continues to heal, Nick is working hard to improve his strength, stamina, energy and dexterity. These are not things you or I can easily see with the naked eye, and they may not be quickly noticed.

The doctor originally thought it would be 8 months before he could be back at his business doing what he had done before. I think it's safe to say that Nick will shave considerable time off that estimate! He has already begun slowly taking over the computer duties there.

He is waiting for his compression suit for his arms, legs and hands to arrive so he can get rid of the temporary ones. He will wear this almost constantly (23 hours a day) for one year.

Nick and Hallie attended a Burn Survivors Support Group function the other evening. There was a fellow burn survivor there who had been released from the burn unit just as Nick came in. He talked to Nick, and told him that he had kept tabs on his condition and recovery process. I thought that was awesome. Those two guys have a connection that was formed only from both surviving a horrific ordeal. And now they reach out to each other...

Nick's mom

From our Blog: Thursday, September 30, 2010 7:45 AM, EDT

I have been waiting for Nick to post about this, but now I am simply BURSTING!!!! He is still going for PT/OT and just saw the surgeon, the wonderful Dr. McCollum, this past Monday. The doctor's initial estimate was 8 months before he would be able to be back to his business 100%. Well...They told Nick that he is about 4 months ahead of the average patient! He has already taken back over all of the office duties and is starting to get into the manual stuff. There have still been some volunteers coming in on heavier days, but Nick is TAKING HIS LIFE BACK!!!! Did we have any doubt he would?

The doctor and therapists are amazed by Nick. His recovery rate is due in part to the level of physical fitness he had before the accident and good nutrition. But that's only part of it. He is tenacious at performing his PT workouts and has even worked in running to his routine. If any of you have ever had surgery where PT was a requirement afterward, you know just how hard it is to exercise and stretch when it hurts. Most often, patients slack off on this very important step, make excuses as to why they don't have to go into PT, and even cut back on the number of required reps of each exercise. Not our Nick. If he was told to do an exercise ten times, he did twelve times. If he had to do twenty reps, he did twenty-five. This was key in getting his range of motion back.

I am so proud of my boy! Not only for his physical accomplishments, but for his attitude and courage throughout these past two months. Hallie has been right there beside him with her love and encouragement the whole way. There are so many blessings in this, and we are so grateful....

Nick's Mom

From our Blog: Thursday, September 30, 2010 9:36 AM, EDT

Hello, it's Nick again. I was actually going to post but my mom beat me to it. So I will leave you with this: Recovery-the worst part is what got you there, the best part is defying the odds and expectations.

PS: A coach once told me "mind over matter" this is the truth. Maybe I'm hard-nosed, maybe I have a high tolerance for pain, but mind over matter really works. When you want something, go get it, don't let it sit there just out of reach. If you push hard enough you will have it in your hands. Never let your spirits get down.

Nick

From our Blog: Friday, October 8, 2010 2:01 PM, EDT

And Nick continues to improve and amaze us all as he goes along! He went to his PT/OT today and due to his fantastic progression, next Friday will be his last appointment! He will be carrying on with his daily workouts just like he was doing before all of this happened. I picture this news as another checkmark on Nick's Personal Recovery Checklist...Complete Physical and Occupational Therapy --- Check!

Are you marveling at the speed of Nick's recovery? Most people are. Many have been inspired by Nick's story. This entire process is a testament to his attitude. He just does not allow himself to get down. I'm sure he's had his moments; he wouldn't be human if he didn't. But he's been to hell and back and is a stronger man for it. "CAN'T" just isn't in his vocabulary.

NICK SPEAKS OUT 2

Nick, What do you remember about the accident?
All I really remember is that I was working in the boat, and then I heard a boom. I didn't see anything but a flash of orange and I shut my eyes and dove. I saw where I thought the fire was above the boat. The next thing I realized, I was on the ground. There is only a two-foot area between the boat and the wall of the garage. How I made it from where I was, I don't know. For me to get from the boat to the floor in one shot, I would say is a pretty tough chance given I couldn't see anything. I had shut my eyes. I remember just diving. I remember feeling assisted. I don't mean being blown out of the boat from the explosion; this was a feeling of being lifted. The next thing I knew I was on the ground. In between the dive and getting to the ground I don't know what happened. I mean, to get from the center of the boat where I was in one fell swoop to the ground without severe burns to my face, I know without a doubt that someone was there helping me get out of that boat. As bad as my burns were with my face not getting burned, the only logical explanation is someone had to cover my face. I believe it was my angel.

My doctor actually said that there is no medical explanation for my face not being burned. He said based on the burn patterns, my face should have been burned! I told you, it was my angel.

When I hit the ground, my instinct was to get out. I ran and jumped in the pool, not knowing if I was on fire or not. I really don't know if jumping in the pool helped or not. I honestly feel jumping in the pool did help in the sense it eases the pain when you burn your hand and you immediately run it under cold water. My mom always told me that. I remember her always saying if I burn myself on the stove to run it under cold water. So when I dove in that pool maybe that helped cool the skin down. I was pretty much in a haze after that. I remember going in the house, grabbing my phone and trying to dial 9-1-1. I don't think I really dialed it.

After I came back out of the house, I went back in the pool. The wind hurt after I was in the pool a minute. It started to hurt, so I don't know if that helped cool the skin even more. At that point some neighbors came over and pulled me away from the garage. It was getting worse. I remember the ambulance getting there and someone asking if I could walk. I said I could. The pain factor hadn't set in. I think I was in shock. I knew I was burned because it hurt when the wind blew, but I don't really think I knew how bad it was.

When I got into the ambulance, they basically hit me with Morphine® as much as I could take to diffuse the pain until we got to the hospital. I remember giving Hallie's phone number to a neighbor. I was coherent enough to know what was going on and remember asking an ambulance attendant how bad he thought it was. In my mind I knew I had a couple of weddings I had planned to get to. I hoped he could tell me the severity. But he just looked at me and didn't answer. I took that to mean it might be pretty bad.

I remember the ambulance missing the turn to the hospital and backing up before pulling in. By the time I got to the hospital I pretty much had all four shots of morphine I was allowed. Once the IV was in my arm, they kept it coming. I was sitting covered in blankets, and the pain was starting to set in. They kept asking me what happened, and I was starting to get fuzzy. I remember when I was in the tub room and they asked if it was ok if Hallie, my Mom and Skip came in. At that point I knew you all wanted to know I was alright. But I wanted covered so none of you would see the extent of everything. The only other thing I remember before the mega drugs hit was their asking if I had a will. I freaked out. I said "What are you talking' about, a will? Am I gonna die?" They explained that it was a standard question and tried to calm me down. After everybody left the room, I don't remember anything until I was in my room I would be occupying for a little bit of time. They hit me with a drug that makes you forget. They cleaned me up and did whatever they had to do to treat it. I didn't even know I was on the third floor. I thought I had just rolled right into one of the ER rooms from the ambulance.

When did you realize that you would be in the hospital for a while?
It's all a haze. Then when I heard forty to sixty days it was like a punch in the stomach. Just thinking of being in one room for even three weeks was hard, but forty to sixty days was like a blow to the gut. I thought to myself, "I'm not going to be able to do anything stuck here". At that point I told myself, "It is what it is." I told myself to keep my spirits high and I will come out of it. I just tried to keep my spirits up with the best attitude given the situation and told myself things would work itself out.

What do you remember about your food intake at first?
I remember them saying how much I had to eat and thinking it was totally absurd. 3500-4000 calories a day! I normally eat a lot, and I'm active, but 3500 calories a day! I wasn't sure I could eat

that much, that's a lot of food. If I ate McDonalds three times a day, then maybe I'd get there. But I don't eat fast food. Generally I watch what I buy and what I eat so eating maybe 2500 healthy calories a day was possible. But 3500? 4000? That much food was crazy. I didn't know how I could do that. When the feeding tube went in, it sucked. But at least then I knew I really only had to eat three meals a day, and I was getting the nutrients I needed in order to heal. I didn't have to worry about stuffing my face. It's so much harder knowing you have to eat that much. It's like trying to do a 20-pound steak challenge. You will be psyching yourself out the whole time you know you have to do it and it makes it that much harder.

Do you remember Hallie working with you on getting adequate protein?

She was very good. I couldn't have done it without her. She moved in to the hospital while I was there. I would have assumed most wives would do that, but then again many of the others didn't stay. She was pretty strict and made sure I did everything I had to do. She MADE SURE. She would make me drink additional protein beginning at breakfast. She'd say, "You have to drink it; you have to get your protein." She would put it in anything imaginable, yogurt, shakes, juice, pudding; she'd put it in anything it could be mixed into. On top of that I was drinking milk with extra protein. Mom and Hallie bought out the supply at several Marc's® stores! I ended up taking in a ton of protein because I had the feeding tube in as well. I just know Hallie made sure I was eating my heart out.

What do you remember about the four days of surgeries?

I really don't remember much. I mean it's very, very foggy. I just know I wasn't allowed to drink after midnight, which sucked the most. I'd wake up with only an hour before the deadline and try to drink as much as I could. After the surgery I'd be out of it the rest of the day. I don't remember any visits during those four days. It's pretty much a blur.

Other than the obvious pain and discomfort, what was most upsetting to you during this time?

Having to watch everybody go through seeing me the way I was, Hallie, Mom, Skip, David, Marcy, Dad, DeeAnn, and my friends. Nobody wants to see their friend or loved one in a situation like that. I didn't want to see myself in that situation. When people came in, sometimes they didn't know what to expect. At first I had bandages on my face. They didn't know how bad it was, and they would think it was way, way, way worse, you know? We pretty much didn't know how well I was gonna be. Plus I felt bad because two of my good friend's weddings were coming up, and I was not going to being able to make them. I wanted to be there and couldn't be, and I was disappointed about that.

Halle was stressed out of her mind. I don't even really know what she went through but I kind of do. I know it was very hard on her. I felt bad for the animals at home. They didn't know what the heck was going on. I especially didn't want everyone to be upset. I didn't think of all of the bad things. I tried to stay as positive as I could. I remember one time my friend, Jessie, came in. He later told me he came in not knowing what to expect with my head wrapped up, and he hated to see me that way. Then he said I cracked some kind of joke and he knew I was going to be alright because I was pretty much being my old self.

If you found yourself awake during the night, what was going through your mind?

"There's nothing on TV. The bed's too small. I can't roll over. I need to get out of here I have to go to the bathroom in a pot on the bed", which was horrible. I knew that I couldn't even get out of bed. I just tried to sleep which is kind of hard in a hospital because they poke and prod you every couple of hours. As soon as you try to get good sleep it is time for blood pressure or time for pills, time to do this, or do that, yep, they're in there. There was nothing on TV, and I'd stare into space hoping I would get better faster. I remember having to have my arms irrigated. For some reason I kind of craved the soaking water. Every time they did that I closed my eyes and imagined I was in the cool air or in the sun and it helped a little, my doing that.

What did you take the most comfort in during your hospital stay?
People being there all the time, Hallie, Mom. I wasn't left alone. Sometimes it was stressful to get a lot of visitors. It was very comforting, looking back. It helped knowing I had the support that I had. Knowing how much support there really was with reading the posts is very humbling. You don't know the community you live in until something bad happens. All of these people you don't really know all of a sudden doing all they can to help you. Pretty awestruck from that.

Tell me your mindset once the surgeries were behind you...
Well at that point, I mean my range of motion was shit, pardon my language. I couldn't raise my arms. I wasn't allowed out of bed at first and they would come in and stretch me. They would have me do things like wiggle my toes, flex my fingertips to my thumbs and make fists. At first I thought I could always do some stretches while I lay there. So I stretched my fingers, made fists, pumped my feet back and forth like I was working a gas pedal to get movement. I figured it can't hurt; it's only going to help. I kept doing that. I moved around in bed as much as I could.

What about your first steps, walking...explain your mindset and determination in these areas...

Physical Therapy came every day. I remember the day they told me, "Tomorrow we are going to get you out of bed". They sat me up. I didn't know how hard it would be to sit up. I remember they had me stand real easy. I just stood there going back and forth. They said I would feel some pressure. They wanted to know if I wanted to lie back down or go to the chair. I thought what the heck, I've been in that bed for so long, and I didn't want to be in that bed anymore. I took some steps, wobbly steps, but I took steps across the room and sat down in the chair, a nice accomplishment. Most people would just sit back down after standing and not even take a walk, so that was my thing to get into the chair and be more lively when people came in the next day.

The next day physical therapy came, same deal. They said "We're going to get you up to stand and try to walk today, maybe make it to the doorway". They said it was typically normal to get to the door. My thoughts were "I'm up and walking, and I'm not stopping at the doorway. I'm going to walk as far as I can until my legs feel like I'm ready to fall".

Well I walked down the hall and around the corner; farther than they expected me to go. Hallie followed behind with the wheelchair, and then she wheeled me back into the room. After that I pretty much started to walk more and more every day. Once I was able to get out of bed, I told myself, "I'm up as much as possible!" I refused to be in bed during the day. I sat in the chair, took walks, and I remember beginning the next day, I made a full lap around the unit. After that I did more and more laps.

I just kept walking and trying to not use both hands on the walker. I wanted to see what my balance was to help push me along a little further. I would never just try to do the minimum, I always did more to push it as much as I could to get my strength back and get the heck out of there. I didn't want to be there any longer than I had to. I loved being able to move around. Being able to go into the bathroom was a huge relief. And I was determined once I got up in the morning that I was not going to go back into that bed until I was going to sleep at night.

Tell me about the day you went home
Well, in order to be able to go home I had to be able to eat enough on my own so they could take out the feeding tube, handle the tub room without the drugs, have my pain under control with pills instead of IV drugs, be able to go to the bathroom on my own and have the strength to walk and do stairs.

I had the bathroom part down, and I was doing really good on the walking. I had made progress. The first day they let me go outside felt great. It made me feel like a person again. They gave me a shirt and scrub shorts to wear. Hallie and I sat together in the shade and just smiled.

Another thing I liked was being able to eat in the cafeteria. Not being stuck in my room with a tray in front of me was really nice. I was walking a lot; and the nurses were pretty much amazed by everything, how good the healing was going. When I was in the treatment room and they unwrapped my arms, it felt so good. It was such a good feeling to not have the bandages on all the way up. It was very refreshing with everything coming off, and I started to feel better.

The doctors and nurses couldn't believe how fast I was healing. They were looking at my arms at not even three weeks after the accident and were pretty amazed. I was still going to the tub room every day. There were lots of times I didn't remember the tubs. But toward the end of my stay I did remember because I was getting less and less drugs. I would talk to the nurses and ask when they thought I could get out of there. They had said maybe in a week, depending on how I do. I had to prove I could do the tub room without the drugs. I already had transitioned to pills for pain control during the day. Plus I had to be able to go up and down stairs. So with Hallie right there, I did the steps. I had to hold onto the rail, but I showed them I could do it. I was wobbly but Physical Therapy was there guiding me so I didn't fall.

I also had to be able to eat enough calories on my own to get rid of the feeding tube. I remember it was a Sunday and one of my doctor's partners came in. I asked him when I could get the tube out. He said, "Well, I have to make sure you can eat. I don't want to have to put it back. The last thing I want to do is replace that tube". So he said he would look at the numbers again. So about two hours later I was out in the hall walking, and a nurse smiled and said, "Good news! I got the order to take your tube out!" That was a real victory for me. It proved that I can do what I set my mind to.

Now that's where Hallie came back in with monitoring the eating again. Before they removed the tube I had been eating during the day, and they fed me through the tube at night. Now it was all on me. Hallie made sure I got every bit of nutrition possible from every which way possible. I remember that first day of eating on my own I was so full I felt like food was backed all the way up my throat. The next day we found out I was 1000 calories over what I needed! Hallie did a good job of making sure I ate.

I remember the night before I ended up going home; I was thinking I should be getting out of here soon. My doctor was on vacation until the weekend so I figured I couldn't go home until he came back. So I thought the weekend was a good guess. That night as I was trying to sleep, I got poked and prodded like always. Finally I fell asleep. A nurse woke me up early in the morning and the first thing out of her mouth was "We're going to try to get you home today!" What?! I had been sleeping hard and was in a haze. I remember thinking, "Am I dreaming?" Hallie and I were on cloud nine. It was the news we'd wanted to hear but didn't think we were going to get for another 30 days. All of a sudden getting that news early was really awesome. Being able to get out of there was a good feeling.

The Homecoming...

I didn't really know the extent of the damage to the garage until I got home. But it really didn't bother me. I was so excited to get home and be home. It was so nice to be able to go outside and have the comfort of my own house. It was also nice not to have to worry about people coming into my bedroom in the middle of the night! I was a little worried about how my dog, Brody, would react when he saw me. But he was fine. I think he knew something was going down. He was pretty gentle. It was a big relief getting home.

Oh, and the hospital breathing machine. I had to breathe into it to keep my lungs strong. I hated that stupid machine. I had to do it every hour on the hour, and I hated doing it really bad. Mom and Hallie, mainly Mom, made sure I did it. When that minute hand hit the hour it was in my face, and I wanted to punch that thing out. When I was going home the nurse handed me the breathing machine and said, "This is yours". I didn't want that thing in my house. Hallie probably kept it.

Early days

When I first got home, the bandage on my back was a rubbery thing that couldn't be changed until I went back to my outpatient appointment a week later. Having it on really sucked. I couldn't fully bathe, so Hallie had to give me sponge baths. I couldn't get my torso wet. I would get really hot with all of that extra stuff around my waist. It was a pain in the butt working around it, trying not to mess it up with my shirt and everything. My back was really sore. It was still pretty raw since I had been lying on it all that time. It hadn't healed, so getting up and down was tough. I couldn't change positions that fast and when I did, it hurt. But it was nice to be able to go outside and just sit there. It made a big difference. Once I healed a little more, the dressing changes weren't so bad except for a couple of areas on my legs that still needed wrapped. It was just a process.

Because of the grafts, my body temperature control was out of whack. I was hot, I was cold. It was so out of whack. So I'd be super-hot, then super-cold. Having all of that stuff around my torso made a big difference too. Hallie bought me tennis shoes for my first physical therapy appointment. She didn't want me going in flip flops. That was the first real time I went out. It was about one week after being released from the hospital. We went to my first doctor's visit and to PT, and they took all the stuff off of my back. Then they re-wrapped it with regular bandages. Afterwards, Hallie wanted to give me a little change of scenery so we went out to eat. That was real nice.

During that first PT appointment, I used an elliptical to hang and stretch my arms to help get my range of motion back. By then it was almost completely back, but after that visit I could get my arms all the way up. That first time they had to stretch me for awhile, and then I did the apparatus at home to stretch. I would do those exercises every day. At the second PT appointment, I hung on the elliptical and also started using the bike and the treadmill. From then on at PT, I was hanging for longer periods. My grip strength was weak, about half of what it had been. My therapist asked if I was walking, which I was. She suggested trying to jog.

It was so nice when Hallie and I went for the first walk. It was just great to be able to go for a walk just right in front of our house. We walked every day. We would walk down the hill then back up. Then we went all the way around and did a lap. I walked more and more every day. Hallie would encourage me to even jog here and there. The first day I was on a walk by myself I was feeling good, so I tried to jog a little intermittently. I came to a hill around the corner and thought to myself, "I'm going to give it a shot!" I actually jogged the hill! I was pretty much wiped out after that, but accomplishing that was really nice.

In PT my therapist upped the levels when I told her what I had been doing. More and more of my strength was coming back. They were all just dumbfounded and said I was six months ahead of the game. My range of motion came back really fast because of how hard I was working. I had it back after my third visit. Most times patients are still getting stretched but at their third visit. I was working out instead of just getting stretched. Because I was doing more and more, she was giving me harder stuff to do. And I kept doing it. She was just amazed.

I started to tweak the exercises on paper. I started doing push-ups. I had to start on my knees, but I found little ways to do more. I worked really hard. I wanted to get back to, who I was as fast as possible. I didn't want to hold out. I thought I probably wasn't going to be able to ski that first winter, which was something I really liked to do. My therapist, said it was probably ok, just to take it easy. When I heard that, I kept working harder and harder. I skied, and I didn't take it easy! The first couple of times I went out skiing, I was noticeably weaker in my main muscles. I needed to ski to keep working out and getting stronger. By the end of the season my strength was not quite what it was, but it is getting there. Next year it will probably be back to what it was.

One day during one of our walks, Hallie and I stopped in at the Greentown Fire station to see if anybody happened to be there that was on the call the day of the accident. The captain looked in the call log and said one of the guys was there, so I got to thank him in person.

I told him that I wanted to pop in and thank all the guys for coming to my rescue. He asked how I was, and we talked a little bit. It was nice stopping in there to show my gratitude.

Tell me about your business...

Note: *Nick's business, Advanced Fulfillment Solutions in Tallmadge, Ohio gets orders into the hands of customers quickly and efficiently. He receives an electronic label from his clients, which is adhered to the package. The specific product is inserted and everything is transferred cost effectively for nationwide delivery. His company handles over twenty different products and assorted accompanying materials.*

It was so upsetting to not be able to work for so long. It disappointed me the most because I owned my own business, and I wasn't able to go to work. I felt like I was letting everybody down. I didn't know what was going to happen. It was hard not being able to do anything and not knowing the day-to-day happenings. Little did I know how many people would jump out of the woodwork to keep my business open. It was really something. Including Mom, how she handled things was really amazing. Once I got home from the hospital, it was so nice to get back into work and dive my nose back into things. It just felt great to get a grasp on what was going on.

At home early on after I got released, I was pretty wiped out. Later on, even though I couldn't go in and do the actual work, I was able to go into the office while the helpers did the actual labor. I just did some paperwork and got my accounting caught up, which was awesome-not! Later as the labels came in, I wanted to try to put them on. I couldn't grab the boxes and carry them, so I brought small stacks from boxes instead. My speed wasn't really affected, but I had to be more careful how I did things at first so I didn't get paper cuts. It felt good to be able to do the work. When I got to the point where I could load everything myself, it helped my grip strength. So I would just get going more and carry more mailbags. Holding on to the bags helped my grip strength. Finally being able to do the work was nice.

I couldn't drive at all at first. But it didn't take long. I was back to driving about two weeks after I got home, like the beginning of October. I started out slow. The original doctor's estimate was that I wouldn't be able to go back to work until March. He didn't think I'd heal that fast. But I thought to myself, "I'm not doing that", not working until March I mean. Being back to work two months after being released from the hospital is pretty darn good. The doctor was astounded by that.

Eight months after the accident...

The compression suit is a skin colored garment designed to prevent keloids, the bumps on the skin. At first I wore them on my arms, hands, legs and feet almost constantly. I only wear the gloves now all the time. I take them off for a little while when I'm at home. I wear the arms only when I wear short sleeves. I don't wear any of them during the night or during my workouts. My skin tone is pretty much all back to normal. There is no raising of the skin. My therapist wants me to keep wearing the garments, but guesses that by May I will not have to wear them at all anymore. I'm really tired of wearing it. My skin isn't going to be perfect like it used to be. But it won't get any worse than it is now. I know from looking at it every day. If it hasn't risen by now it's not going to rise. I don't want this stuff on.

I feel 100%. Whether my skin is 100% I don't know, probably not. But the way my strength feels is pretty much where it was. My grip is fine. I work out now like I normally did before the accident. I dropped back some as I don't need to lift for size; I just want to stay in shape. I work out now like nothing happened. It was a bump in my road that I brushed off my shoulder, and I'm back to what I was doing.

Lessons taken from all this...

Always be aware when around gasoline and fumes. Be careful with what you're doing. Looking back, I shouldn't have done anything with the boat until the gas tank was out of there. You think of gas being flammable, but you don't think about the vapor. I learned that the vapor is the worst part of gas. Knowing what I know now, I will take my precautions if I'm dealing with something with a gas tank. If I ever buy another boat, I'll get one I don't have to fix! That and I'll take the gas tank somewhere. I'll take the necessary safe steps. That was a lesson learned to be aware of vapor. It's just as bad as a puddle of gasoline, if not worse.

What about emotional strength?

The main lesson with a patient in the hospital is to keep your spirits up. Just fight. Fight and crawl, and do what you can to get better as fast as you can. Do what the doctor says plus more. Do what you can. I knew that I could do more than they were telling me. Everyone knows their own breaking point. Push yourself to that breaking point.

How can your experience help others?

I hope my attitude that I kept throughout everything will help other people. The other advice I can give is this: When you're down, whether you're hurt or not, if you're not able to do something or people tell you that you can't, push on. Don't listen. Fight to do what you know you can accomplish. Do everything you believe that you have in you to do. When things happen I think it really is a test of the kind of person you are. How you go through your hardships says a lot about you. Will you let something big you are going through overcome you? Take advantage of you? I could have been grumpy and pooh-poohed everything they told me I had to do. Well, then I probably would have been in the hospital for sixty days. But I chose to get out of there as fast as I could and try harder each day. The lesson is never give up.

THE AMISH "BARN RAISING"... AND OTHER LABORS OF LOVE

3

Y   ou don't realize just how much goodness there is in people
     until you are on the receiving end of the kindness. From
     the minute the word got out about Nick's accident, there
was an outpouring of support. Calls, emails, cards, prayer lists,
hugs, food and solidarity. People I didn't even know reached out
to our family.

My friend for many years, Pat Riley, was overcome at the news.
She actually collected donations for the Nick Fund from several of
her clients including Darlene Milavickas, who gave $100. Imagine
that! $100 to a total stranger! Others donating through Pat were Mary
Lousoff, Debra Craig, Deborah Shaffer, Mary Bucklew, Mary Lou
Moretz, Emma Green and Valarie Albaugh. This is a shining example
of true selfless giving.

Our former neighbors, Karen and Galen Miller, came over and
did some yard work for us during the early days. They were joined by
neighbors Jeanette and Ken Mueller who made a donation, Phil and
Kathy Shank who made sure the yard was mowed, Marianne Leake
and her daughter and son-in-law, Andre and Chris Povroznik, who

took on some repairs. These and all of the other angels who helped in any way helped make our days a little brighter.

All of our friends with The Buckeye Cruisers, with who we have enjoyed many enjoyable camping experiences, made a donation to the Nick Fund. Every year the club makes a donation to a worthy cause. This year they decided that the cause would be helping Nick. Sometimes you just don't realize what it means to have good friends until you are on the receiving end of their support.

From our Blog: Saturday, August 14, 2010 2:17 PM, EDT

What began as the brainchild of Joni Miller turned out to be the first public gathering to reach out to Nick and his family. The community response was overwhelming! Never before has a bake sale raised this much money!

My husband, Skip, and I stopped at the bake sale a little after 9AM on the way to the hospital. I had expected to find a couple of card tables of sweets offered for sale. Wow, was I wrong! There were 3 eight-foot tables set up in the front of the store and 2 more in the back of the store, all laden with baked goods. There was a stockpile of additional goodies waiting to take the place of what perched on the tables. All of the baked goods were donated, a plethora of pies, cakes, cookies, brownies, cupcakes and assorted treats. Donated pizza and hot dogs were sold as well. Smack dab in the middle of one of the tables in the front of the store, stood a large container with a picture of Nick's smiling face. It was a donation jar! I stood watching the hum of activity in shock. Tears flowed as so many I didn't even know embraced me and expressed their wishes and prayers for Nick's recovery. Hallie also experienced the same outpouring of support when she visited the sale later in the day. It was a wonderful feeling, a wonderful day.

From our Blog: Saturday, August 14, 2010 7:27 PM EDT

Joni came to the hospital on Monday and presented Nick and Hallie with the proceeds from the bake sale. I will just say, it was a good thing we were all sitting down! Joni said she has never seen a bake sale produce results such as this-ever. The entire community came together and gave and gave and then they bought and bought. An ENORMOUS thank you to the vendors who contributed, first of course Hartville Hardware, also Hartville Printing (posters), Romeo's Pizza (pizza), Pizza Hut (pizza, breadsticks), Duma's Meats (10 pounds hot dogs) Euro Gyro (baklava), Giant Eagle (gift card for drinks and buns), Walnut Creek Cheese House ($25 for baked goods), Hartville Chocolate Factory (caramel puffs and paper products), Frontier Restaurant (muffins), AVI Fresh (muffins, bread, cookies), Hartville Mennonite Church (donated money earned from leftover bake sale items), Speedway (ice), Yoder Medical (baked goods), Best Cuts (baked goods), Miss Pink Cupcakes (cupcakes) plus volunteers: Greg Davis (Joni's hubby), Bob & June Miller (Joni's parents) Cindy Wright, Zach Miller, Ashley Adams, Autumn Nichols, Darlene Giffin, Sylvia Short, Charlene Yoder, Betty Miller, Betty Yoder, Sharon Lam, Brian and Jody Miller, Justin and Morgan Miller, Amanda Miller, Patty Miller, The Beall Family, Nate Searle, anyone who baked, anyone who bought or who helped in any other way! Nick's Family THANKS YOU, LOVES YOU AND SENDS YOU WISHES FOR GOD'S BLESSINGS!

From our Blog: Saturday, August 14, 2010 7:28 PM, EDT

Hi Nick, I was at the bake sale all morning, and I just want to tell you that the love and support of the community for you is truly amazing. We had four tables stacked with baked goods, behind and underneath the tables, and the food just kept coming all morning! Your mom and I stood there and cried when we saw the generosity poured out for you. A lot of people saw the article in the Hartville News and came down just because of that. They wanted to help and let you know they were praying for you. What a blessing for our great community! Your strength, courage and determination inspire us to strive toward a higher level. You set a high standard for all of us to reach for! We pray for your continued progress and speedy healing.

Darlene Giffin

From our Blog: Wednesday, August 25, 2010 8:50 AM, EDT

We want to thank Danyell Bloomer who has been making gift baskets full of Paul Mitchell Products and placing them for sale at her Bella Sorella's Hair & Nail Salon (which means Beautiful Sisters in Italian). She donated the proceeds to the Nick Fund. Great Idea for a fundraiser and very much appreciated! Danyell and her husband, Nick, are neighbors of Nick and Hallie, but they hadn't met until this accident. Nick Bloomer was on the scene the day of the fire.

From our Blog: Tuesday, September 21, 2010 8:47 AM, EDT

wow Wow WOW! The Golf Outing held this past Saturday at Sable Creek Golf Course was nothing short of AMAZING! We had 120 golfers tee off to the shotgun start for the scramble that started at 1:30PM. Guess who took the first tee shot on hole number one? None other than Nick himself! I was standing by with my camera and took plenty of pictures you can be sure of that! Then the golfers took off and Nick and Hallie took it easy for awhile.

About thirty more arrived for dinner at 6PM and enjoyed pasta, courtesy of PAPA BEARS, chicken and jojos, courtesy of SMITHS WACO MARKET, pie, courtesy of FISHER FOODS and soft drinks courtesy of PEPSI. All the signs were courtesy of STANDARD PRINTING. THANK YOU!!!!

A Skins Game collected $456 and there was only one skin won by the team of Lee DiCola, Dave DiCola, Jimmy DiCola and Marty. They VERY GENEROUSLY **DONATED BACK their ENTIRE WINNINGS TO NICK!!!! All $456 of IT!!! THANK YOU!!!!**

The overall generosity was incredible. We had 18 hole sponsors at $100 a hole. There were lots of other businesses and individuals who donated prizes that were donated for the raffle. After dinner the winners were announced. We sold tickets and 100% of the proceeds went to Nick and Hallie.

Last but most certainly not least, my son, David, put this entire outing together and did a superb job. He had never put a golf outing together before, but this was done like he had been doing it for a living. It was top notch, and everyone said so. He stepped up because he loves his brother. He saw a need and did everything in his power to make it happen. Even the Lord made the most beautiful weather day sandwiched in between nasty rainy days to help make the day perfect. I was never prouder of my David then I was during this time. You did good.

Nick's mom

From our Blog: Tuesday, October 5, 2010 3:40 PM, EDT

AMAZING was the word for the turnout for the Pasta Dinner this past Sunday! There were people who sent in reservations and/ or donations that don't even know Nick and Hallie. We were all overwhelmed by the showing of generosity and support. The food was great! There was a Game Station for the little ones that was a BIG HIT! Nick and Hallie were there the whole time, and Nick even made a little speech. I told you he had a talent for speaking!!! **THANK YOU's** are in order to...Emidio & Sons Restaurant who donated half of the pasta, Lee & Dorothy DiCola who donated the other half of the pasta plus the chicken and bread, Laura Kulwicki who donated the salads, beverages and photo buttons, and Cherie Grescovich who donated the desserts, paper products and game supplies. Also a huge Thank You to Cherie for the planning and organization of the event. It was Top Notch. Cherie also had wrist bands made that say **NICK...EXCEPTIONAL... PERSEVERE.** They came from wristbandswithamessage.com and they donated 200 of them, which was half of the total order. They were done in dark blue and gold, Notre Dame Colors, Nick's favorite team. At the event there were activities for children as well as a 50/50 drawing. Cherie even featured Nick's favorite beverage, Californians! Thanks also to everyone who helped in any way. We are so grateful, more than words can ever say. Blessings to all!

Nick's Mom

From our Blog: Friday, October 8, 2010 2:01 PM, EDT

Another example of others taking Nick into their hearts is this: On Sat, Oct 16th volunteers and friends of Maple Grove Mennonite Church will converge at Nick & Hallie's house and proceed to rebuild a new garage, all in one day! Insurance provided materials and this generous, good-hearted group is donating their labor! It's going to be like an "Amish Barn Raising"! I am coordinating the food effort to feed this wonderful group of guys! With me in there handling food quantity, you know we won't be running out of food! Can't wait!

Nick's mom

From our Blog: Tuesday, October 19, 2010 7:59 AM, EDT

Have you ever witnessed a miracle? I did on Saturday...

Do you know what an "Amish barn raising" is? I've seen the movie "Witness". All the Amish folk come together and build a barn for one of their community members that have the need. The women cook and serve the food and drink to the men midway through. I always thought this sojourn of sprit nothing short of a miracle, to see a barn standing at the end of the day where only open field existed that morning. But never did I think I would experience such a thing first hand...

On Saturday, October 16, 2010 volunteers and friends from Maple Grove Mennonite Church in Hartville, Ohio converged on this small tract of land in Uniontown, Ohio to offer their hands, sweat, strength and love to rebuild the garage that Nick and Hallie lost in the fire. I've never before witnessed anything so powerful...

I never saw anything like it nor is it likely I ever will again. At 7:30 AM, 20 angels converged on the site of what was once a burned out garage. They worked like little bees in complete sync with each other. They called out measurements, saws rang out, and it was the coolest thing. I ran all around taking pictures from all directions. All four sides of the new garage formed. It was complete magic.

I watched the crane lifting roof trusses three at a time. I was like a child awestruck as they were lifted high in the air then settled softly on the waiting perfect spot. Soon there were no more trusses to be placed and the cranes work was done. Roofers swarmed to do their job as windows were placed. Betty Miller appeared bearing doughnuts, coffee, hot chocolate and orange juice, which provided a break for the guys around 10 AM. Then it was back to work.

The roof was done, the sides and all around in progress when Hallie and I laid out the lunch spread at around 12:30. A mighty feast! Perry Miller of Countryside Plumbing, the organizer of this event said the blessing. Nick expressed his gratitude. Thank you to all who helped us with all the food. I know the guys enjoyed it.

By 4 PM a brand new 4-car garage complete with overhead doors and siding proudly stood on Nick and Hallie's property. A true labor of love had taken place there that day. People who didn't even know Nick and Hallie had taken time away from their families, their own life to give to someone else in need. They are all wonderful people who understand the true power of giving. For it is only in giving that we receive. God sees all that we do and blesses us in turn. God bless all of these guys and their loved ones. Now let's each and every one of us carry it forward.

Nick's mom

About Burns   4

I had never known anyone who had suffered serious burns before Nick had his accident. So the entire process was completely new to me. They say that burns are the most painful injuries that someone endures. I know it is not something you want to witness a loved one going through. I learned a lot.

I found out that the higher the percentage of burns, the higher the mortality rate. Those that suffer 50% of their body being burned often don't survive at all. Nick was at 46%.

According to the burn statistics found at www.burnsurvivor.com, approximately 2.4 million burn injuries are reported every year. Of those, 75,000 require hospitalization. Of that number, 20,000 are considered major burns of at least 25%. Between 8,000 and 12,000 burn victims die. And about one million of those burned have permanent disabilities from their burn injury.

In 1992, injuries from burns were the second leading cause of accidental death after motor vehicle accidents. In 2005, burns were the third leading cause of death.

And the cost to treat? Burns are the most expensive catastrophic injury to treat. For example, someone with burns of 30% of the total body area is looking as high as $200,000 in hospitalization and doctor's costs. If the burns are extensive, there is additional cost for reconstruction surgery, rehab and supplies.[12]

According to the Center for Disease Control (CDC) in Atlanta, GA, most fire victims die from the inhalation of smoke or toxic gas.[13] In Nick's case, I remember the doctors being concerned early on that he had inhaled some of the vapors. The day after his admission they checked his lungs and trachea but they were clear. I knew at the time that they were concerned about it, but I really didn't understand just how serious it was.

According to statistics at www.rescource4burninjury.com, many victims of burn injuries suffer serious psychological trauma that is best treated by counseling and support groups. These resources help the burn survivors return to their lives. This trauma also affects the family members close to the burn victim.[14]

I remember one morning not long after the accident, I was getting dressed and the television was set on the local news. The report flashed to a car explosion that had occurred along the highway. I stood transfixed as I watched the flames and heard the sounds of the explosion and the sirens. I started to shake and had to turn off the television. I kept telling myself "That wasn't Nick, that wasn't Nick." According to the hospital psychologist, this was completely normal. What wasn't normal would be if this type of reaction continued. I was alert to this type of reaction from Nick. Once after everyone had left for the day, he and Hallie were watching a movie. There was a

---

12 Burn Statistics, www.burnsurvivor.com
13 Burn Statistics, Fire Deaths and Injuries Fact Sheet, Center for Disease Control (CDC), Atlanta, GA, http://www.cdc.gov/HomeandRecreationalSafety/Fire-Prevention/fires-factsheet.html
14 Burn Statistics, www.rescource4burninjury.com

fire scene, and Hallie said he never said a word and didn't seem to get visibly shaken. But I also remember that a few of us in the room one day were discussing various aspects of the accident and Nick asked us to stop talking about it. He seemed a bit antsy, and it was then that I realized that hearing the details was causing him to relive it, something he did not want to do. This too was normal.

According to information found at www.ameriburn.org admissions to burn centers have been steadily increasing. This is because it is now recognized that burn patients have special needs, which also requires that those that transport and treat these patients be trained on exactly what to do. Burn centers now average at least 200 admissions compared to 4700 acute care hospital admissions. Less than 3. 66% of these major burns occur at home.[15]

We live within 20 miles of Akron Children's Hospital's Burn Unit. I have lived in this area all of my life yet I never realized that the Burn Unit was there. I'm sure I had heard references to it over the years in news reports about patients being transported to the burn unit but somehow it didn't register with me. I also didn't realize just how specialized burn units were, didn't even know that all hospitals didn't have them. I found out through this experience that the burn unit at Akron Children's Hospital is considered one of the premier units in the entire country. How fortunate we were to live so close!

Akron Children's Hospital is the ninth largest children's hospital in the country by total number of bed count. The hospital originally opened in 1890 as a day nursery.[16]

The hospital's website at www.akronchioldrens.org says that the Paul and Carol David Foundation Burn Institute at Akron Children's Hospital has provided the needed specialized care for burn victims

---

15   Burn Statistics, www.ameriburn.org
16   Hospital Facts, www.ameriburn.org

of all ages since 1978. It is one of only two pediatric hospitals in the entire USA that also treats adult burn patients.

The Clifford R Boeckman M.D. Burn Center, which is part of the Burn Institute, cares for its patients from the moment they arrive through rehabilitation. There is a treatment room, physical therapy room, operating room and tub room, which is very specialized. The 12 private patient rooms include a bathroom and accommodations for one family member to stay.

The expert staff stays up-to-date on the latest in burn research and burn care through training. In 1974, the hospital's own researchers discovered the method for growing human skin in the laboratory. This technique revolutionized burn treatment.

The staff also is very involved in the community by providing preventive programs that teach both children and adults how to avoid burn injuries. This program is called Juvenile Firestoppers. This is an annual event that teaches children the risk of playing with matches and other fire setting activities. Through interactive games, discussions and other activities, children as young as three learn about fire prevention.[17]

Before this accident, I didn't realize the role that skin plays to protect our body. Not having studied physiology or having a nursing background, I just was unaware of the facts. I sure got a crash course, and not in a classroom environment. I discovered that the skin regulates the body's temperature. If enough skin is lost, that ability is gone.[18]

Since Nick's injury was at 46% of his body, he will be dealing with temperature issues for the rest of his life.

He has always loved his air conditioning, hates to be hot. After the accident with his body being unable to cool itself, a few of us got together and had whole house air conditioning installed at Nick and

---

17 Hospital Facts, https://www.akronchildrens.org/cms/about_akron_childrens/index.html and https://www.akronchildrens.org/cms/department/burn_center/
18 Burn Facts, http://www.medicinenet.com/burns/article.htm

Hallie's house. We had planned to do this before he was discharged but it ended up happening a few days later. During the interim, Nick had many fans trained on him, yet the sweat poured from his head. Once it was installed, just seeing his comfort level increased was worth any price that would have had to be paid.

As an extra blessing, the installer (Greg from Accurate Air Flow in East Canton, Ohio) did it for his cost, pulling off his crew from money-making jobs to do this one. I talked to him during the installation, and he told me that his wife was in remission from cancer. He believed with his whole heart that we all need to give back which is why he was donating his time and profit. What a man.

When someone suffers a burn, the degree of the injury is determined by how deep the burn extends, its location and how much of the body's surface is affected. Since there are three layers of skin, the worst burns are those that burn through to the third layer. The epidermis is the outer layer, the second layer, the dermis, is made up of collagen and elastic fibers that houses nerves, blood vessels, sweat glands and hair follicles. The third layer, the hypodermis, is where the larger blood vessels and nerves are located. It is also where the regulation of body temperature occurs.[19]

We have all heard the terms first, second and third degree burns. I knew that third degree was the worst, but I didn't really understand what the differences were. A first degree burn affects only the outer layer of skin. There is pain, redness and even some swelling. Second degree burns extend deeper into the second layer of skin and include blistering. Third degree burns go even deeper, damaging nerves and blood vessels and actually kill that area of skin. They have a white, even leathery appearance.

I also didn't know that burn patients are watched closely as the burns tend to move deeper after the initial burn. Only the first layer of

19 Burn Facts, http://www.medicinenet.com/burns/article.htm

skin can regenerate. The others cannot and often results in scarring and permanent injury with skin that won't return to normal functioning.

In determining the percentage of the total body area affected by the burn, it depends where the burn is located. Nick was burned from the knees down on both legs including the tops of both feet. He was also burned on both arms including the tops of his hands. He had flash burns on this face and neck. The total body area affected was determined to be 46%

As the percentage increases, so does the risk of death. Patients with burns covering more than 50% of the body have a significant risk of not surviving. I am so glad that I didn't know this at the beginning!

If more than 20% of the body is burned, significant fluid loss has occurred. The patient often goes into shock. Once admitted to the hospital, intravenous fluids are begun immediately.[20]

The location of the burns is very important. If burns occur on the face, nose, mouth or chest, breathing problems may arise. Luckily Nick only sustained flash burns to his face and neck. The doctor was in awe over this. From a scientific viewpoint while studying the burn pattern, he was at a loss to explain how his face was spared. It was at this point that I pictured an angel placing her wings over his face to protect him. I believe!

While Nick didn't have burns in a location to obstruct his airway, all of his limbs sustained major burns. I found out later that this could affect blood flow to the area and increase the chances of losing those limbs. His odds were improved because the palms of his hands and the bottoms of his feet weren't burned.

Flexation became a very important part of his day to prevent the shortening of the muscles. And when he was awake, he was fanatic about doing his stretching exercises.

---

20 Burn Facts, http://www.medicinenet.com/burns/article.htm

Throughout Nick's hospital stay, we had to be vigilant about infection. We even stopped visitors during this critical time. The skin is the organ that keeps viruses and infection out of the body. Since Nick had lost 46% of his body's skin, he was at high risk for infection. This we could not allow. The last thing anyone wanted to do was endanger Nick and his recovery, but most times we don't think that our little sniffles could be harmful. We used plain language in restricting visitors on our daily blog. Everyone was happy to do their part in keeping Nick's recovery going in the right direction.

We were also grateful that Nick had his age, health and physical fitness on his side. It helped him to defy the odds. The grueling week of four skin graft surgeries included four separate anesthesia's, four days in a row. Difficult to watch, but even harder to endure. I often wondered how someone older or less physically fit could have handled it. I was told sometimes the patient is kept unconscious throughout all of the days of the graft surgery.

Another common after effect of burn injuries and skin graft surgery is keloids. Those are the scars that appear like bumps on the skin. You may have one from an old surgery site. They are very visible scars that can spread to the surrounding area. Once you have a keloid, they don't go away.

Because of the high risk of keloids, Nick was required to wear a compression suit for one year following the surgeries. This suit covered both arms, hands, legs and feet and is much like the fabric body armor that is worn by athletes during wintertime activities. It is very form fitting and does not breathe much. They are usually flesh colored and completely unnoticeable under clothing. They have to be worn about 23 hours a day even during sleep. Nick is allowed to go without them during his daily workouts to help keep his body temperature from going through the roof!

I learned that the tendency to develop keloids could be hereditary. I was asked if I was susceptible to them. I didn't think that I was, but as it ends up I do have two keloids. One is from a traumatic appendectomy when I was ten. The other is from a fall I took on my bike when I was twelve that really needed stitches but didn't get them. I never thought much about them before, but I am very aware of them now.

Keloids are more likely to form on the chest, back, shoulders and earlobes but can occur in other areas. Those prone to keloids should avoid elective skin surgery or body piercing.[21]

At the eight month mark after the accident, Nicks' burns are healing very nicely. His arms and legs look better than I had ever hoped for with no keloids! His hands and feet are still healing.

21   Burn Facts, http://www.medicinenet.com/burns/article.htm

LIFE LESSONS THROUGH A MOTHER'S EYES

5

As a mother who has gone through the trauma of watching her child suffer, I know there is something to be shared from my experience. Regardless of the source of the trauma, or the age of the child, a mother's feelings are the same. All the moms tend to gravitate toward each other in the hospital waiting rooms, recognizing our own grief and terror in the eyes of the other. We listen to each other's stories, offer comfort and share tears. We become each other's cheerleaders.

The nurses told us from the very beginning that the burn unit was like a roller coaster ride with the highs and the lows. And it definitely was a roller coaster ride. The dread as we crept up the hill, holding our breath as we crested, then the relief as we raced downward into the valley, the twists, the turns, the clench of the stomach as we approached each new rise. The ride seemed never-ending. From watching my son in his hospital bed day after day, this was a thrill ride I wanted to stop.

Through the course of days, there evolved seven lessons. I call them Life Lessons through a Mother's Eyes. They are from my unique vantage point as Nick's Mom but my inspiration was my son.

Lesson Number One: Faith – You Just Gotta...

I couldn't have made it through without faith. The belief and prayers of our large network kept me going during my moments of despair. Faith helps you keep the worry off your face when you need to even if it feels like it is going to burst from you. It keeps you from crumbling into a howling mess of keening misery. It lifts you up when you fall and keeps a steady arm on your elbow as you walk. You may not be able to look ahead into the next day or even to the next minute, but faith will get you through, each second at a time.

When facing any kind of crisis, especially one that affects your child, faith is the essential ingredient. You simply ask God to help you. My words were:

Please Lord, I can't face this alone. I give it up to you. Please protect Nick. Please give Hallie the strength she needs. Please help me be able to help them both.

It is normal to feel anger, shock and despair. So don't feel guilty if you do, even if some of that anger is directed at God. But the important thing is to get past the anger at God and ask for his help. Without his help you will sink into despair. It is incredible the sense of peace that will overtake you when you just Let Go and Let God.

So why is it that bad things seem to happen only to good people? That is perception. When awful things happen to good people we wonder why and cry out about the unfairness of it all. We can probably think of a name or two who, in our estimation, deserves the bad times more. But as much as we may not want to admit or accept, it is through the pain, heartache and hardship that we grow. We learn from the sorrows we endure and often good things come out of our tragedies.

More importantly, none of us are privy to The Plan. We all go through our life experiences for a reason. Sometimes we find out what the reason was and sometimes not. But part of faith is to trust that there is a higher purpose for our suffering. It's the hard times that teach us valuable lessons needed for our journey here on this earth. We don't have to understand it, we just have to trust God and keep the faith. And we have to accept it.

I'm human. I have fought this process at different times in my life. I've raised my fist at God, the universe and everybody in it. But I was unhappy, and so was anyone else who came within three feet of me. Eventually I came around and humbly asked God to do it because I couldn't. It was only then that I found peace.

Eckhart Tolle says it best "Surrender comes when you no longer ask, Why is this happening to me? Accept what is…"[22]

Lesson Number Two: Control—Stay on the Merry-Go-Round
I like being in control. I like to plan and organize everything from the family vacation to the location of the silverware. I plan and plan and then I plan some more. I rarely do things spur of the moment, except maybe go for ice cream. I plan events, errands and even the down time on my calendar. If you live with someone who wants you to take a drive at the spur of the moment to go pick up some obscure item when that is your only downtime of the week, well it's not pretty. You will tend to drive each other nuts!

When illness or injury strikes someone we love, we have no control. We are afraid. It is a terrible, helpless feeling.

Again faith will help. It helps you to be in control even when you're not really in charge at all. It helps you control your emotions and runaway mind. It gives you a dose of serenity to get through each day and all the minutes they contain.

When I'm faced with a situation where I have no control, I arm myself with knowledge. I read everything I can about it. Maybe in

22 *Stillness Speaks*, Eckhart Tolle, 2003 by Eckhart Tolle, New World Library, Novato, CA and Namaste Publishing, Vancouver, Canada.

that way I feel like I'm prepared for what's ahead even if I can't control it. But use caution. With the plethora of information available on the internet, you may get more information than you're ready to see. Move according to your own comfort level, and stop if your anxiety level starts to go up.

At times during Nick's hospital stay I needed incredible amounts of control. I needed not to break down during that initial briefing on the extent of his injuries so I could support Hallie in her fear. I needed not to cry in front of Nick as they wheeled him off to all four of his surgeries. I needed not to get impatient if his pain meds didn't arrive on the dot. Nick would see me getting frantic, and it upset him. Although I have to admit that there was a time or two that I threatened to go all Shirley MacLaine on everyone if they didn't just Give-My-Son-The-Shot!!!!

Sometimes I just had to let myself lose it. I let loose, often on my drives home at the end of the long day. I allowed my tears to fall unchecked in the shower. I would let my guard down in the cafeteria when I was alone. Sometimes all it would take was a hug from one of the many people who loved Nick to shatter me. But then they would hold onto me and help me regain control. That's the key, keep a tenacious grip on that control. And surround yourself with loved ones…and faith. You just have to believe.

Lesson Number Three: Attitude—When it Sucks, You Suck it Up

You have two choices here. Have a positive attitude or have a negative attitude. A negative attitude will keep you angry, depressed and probably not a picnic to be around. A positive attitude will have a calming effect on you and it will spread to everyone around you - including the patient.

I'm not suggesting that you look at your situation with rose colored glasses, just grab onto the good's more than you do the bad's.

I feel incredibly lucky to be Nick's Mom. His attitude from the onset was several notches higher than positive. He was accepting of his situation and everything it entailed. He didn't complain. He didn't whine. He really was the one who helped us all. Think about it, if Nick could maintain a positive attitude while suffering from horrendous pain, shouldn't we be able to respect him enough to do the same thing?

Watching Nick as he faced this crisis on a daily basis with his never wavering attitude helped us to help him. It helped us endure which in turn helped him to endure. He was an inspiration to everyone he came in contact with and even to those that didn't really know him but were following his story.

When the doctor's were concerned about the possibility of pneumonia, a necessary evil was the breathing machine. He hated it. I was the one who watched the clock and gave him the news that it was time, yet again, to breathe into the machine. I knew he hated it, and I hated having to be the one who made him do it. But at the same time I knew how important it was and how serious pneumonia would be at this juncture.

Nick did his breathing exercises without fail. The only thing he asked of me was not to keep giving him advance notice every minute for a full ten minutes before the time for the exercise was upon him. He might not have said it in quite that way, but I got the message. Although I continued to monitor the clock, I didn't speak until it WAS TIME.

Our outlook when it comes to everyday life is really all about the same two choices. Are we going to approach each day with a positive attitude or a negative one? It shouldn't take a traumatic experience to change our outlook, but sometimes that is exactly how it happens.

The next time you are facing a bump in your road, whether it's a squabble with a friend or family member, relationship woes, money matters or career issues, don't let yourself think negatively. What about the following thoughts:

I'm never speaking to her again!
Why can't I find a partner who appreciates me?
I don't have enough money to pay my bills!
It's too hard to make these sales, I'm going to quit!

When this happens, stop yourself in your tracks. Whatever you tell yourself is going to form your attitude.

Instead of thinking, I'm never speaking to her again! Let yourself calm down and the anger subside. Anger will eat you up and cause you harm, physically and emotionally. The longer it goes on, do you know who is really hurt the most by it? You. Mend that fence. If the relationship is truly toxic, go your separate ways.

Instead of thinking, Why can't I find a partner who appreciates me? Change your focus. Don't try so hard, and just be you. Go about your life, and enjoy your hobbies. God has the perfect person for you when you're not even looking for it.

Instead of thinking, I don't have enough money to pay my bills! Analyze where the money is going. Keep an expense journal if need be to find out. Control the frivolous spending. Start thinking thoughts of plenty, not thoughts of need. Think abundance. Change the focus of your thinking from your lack to your blessings. Be thankful for all of them, and share what you have. Be generous with your time, talent and treasure, and you will be rewarded. And your money situation will change. But do it with a genuine heart.

Instead of thinking, It's too hard to make these sales, I'm going to quit! Do you really think anything worth having in this life is easy? Nothing worth having is ever easy; and the more you work towards a particular goal, the sweeter it is when you achieve it. It goes back to attitude. If you tell yourself that it's too hard, you can't do it, then it is and you can't. You will mope around lamenting about how unfair life is and wonder why can Suzie Q do it and you can't? You will develop the ability to be a chronic complainer and suck the sunshine out of every room.

Or…

You will take some time to determine exactly what you really want to do. Next you will develop a list of goals. Then you will create an action plan that spells out step-by-step what you are going to do towards the desired end result. Baby steps. You will not always be successful at every attempt. But you will accept each experience as a learning activity and strive onward. You will not give up. Ever. You will squelch each negative thought and complaining whine as it begins. And you will be amazed at what you can accomplish!

Lesson Number Four: Perseverance — Keep going until the last dragon is gone

To persevere: Webster defines it as: continued effort to do or achieve something despite difficulties, failure or opposition. Wow. That sounds really hard, doesn't it? To continue to try to do something even if it is difficult, even if you fail, even if others try to get you to change your mind. That's where attitude will help you. It will help you to carry on, to persevere even when it's easier not to.

Nick taught all of us the true meaning of the word persevere. He lived it every day from the minute he was brought into the hospital, during the grueling tub treatments, beyond each necessary procedure, throughout the four excruciatingly painful surgeries, to his first painful step and beyond.

He showed us just what he was made of, what a man he was. I was never prouder than I was watching him grit his teeth and face those demons. And he slayed them too, every single one.

My dear niece, Cherie, took the bull by the horns during Nick and Hallie's time of need by organizing a pasta dinner fundraiser. But she went way beyond that. She had bracelets made that said: **Nick...Exceptional...Persevere.** These bracelets were sold as part of the fundraiser. Even before the day of the pasta dinner, her three beautiful daughters took them to school and everyday came home needing more. She was a rock to me during this time and I love her.

In January 2011, Cherie was diagnosed with pancreatic cancer. After the devastation that this diagnosis caused and the ripples of anguish that swept throughout our family, who do you think epitomized the word persevere? Yes, it was Cherie herself.

She faced this ordeal with the grace and acceptance few could muster. She was a rock in the midst of crisis for her children and all her family. She was surrounded by love and support from a tremendous outreach of people. She had an amazing peace and serenity about her. While it broke my heart to see her go through this along with my brother and sister-in-law, faith is what will sustain us.

Postscript: On May 21, 2011 Cherie lost her battle with pancreatic cancer just a little over four months after diagnosis. Please offer up a prayer for her loved ones left behind who miss her so much...

How is it that we can persevere in spite of great odds? Is it luck? Coincidence? Destiny?

I don't think it is any of those. Since I don't believe in coincidences, it certainly isn't that. Luck? I believe we create our own luck in how we deal with our life situations. Destiny? I do believe that everything happens for a reason, and some of us are destined for greatness. But the ability to persevere doesn't come from any of those things in my opinion. I think the ability to persevere comes from attitude, gratitude and faith. Simply put, what we put into our minds will control our thoughts, and our thoughts will determine our actions.

Put good things in and good things will come out. Easy? Never. Worth it? Always.

Lesson Number Five: Take Care of You. Really.

Everyone seemed to be saying to me during the critical days of Nick's hospital stay, Take care of yourself. I would always nod and say, I know, I will. I knew that if I collapsed it would upset Nick, everyone else and do absolutely nobody any good. And quite honestly, there was no way I was going to let myself fall apart. It wasn't even an option, even when that's all I wanted to do.

But I also knew my own body and my limitations. While I was pushing myself to the extreme limit under an almost unbearable amount of stress, I had to make sure I gave my body a chance to rest and replenish.

I tend to get bronchitis a lot. What usually happens is I push myself and push myself, and then I get sick. Then I recover and start all over again.

I have never been the type of person that can just sit still, unless I'm reading. And I read a lot. But I only read at night. That's how I relax myself at the end of every day. It centers me and gets me ready for sleep.

I read mainly non-fiction, and I love to go to the library. I also have a Kindle®, but I limit the books I put on my Kindle® to business. I read the newspaper every day and keep informed on the bestseller list. Often I will come across a magazine or newspaper article about books that catch my attention. I cut out the information about the book title and author and keep them in a little pouch. I don't think I'll ever run out of options of books to read.

When my mother was alive, we used to talk on the phone every single day. She would always ask what I was doing. It used to drive her crazy that I always had an answer for her. She used to say, "Can't you just sit down?" Well, of course I could; and I did when I was folding clothes, mending, playing board games with the kids or reading to them. But to just sit and aimlessly watch television and do nothing? Rarely.

Now that the kids are grown, I still keep very active. I am very conscious of the passage of time. I learned just how far I can push my body, and I made some changes. For instance, I don't run around every day at lunchtime doing errands. I prefer to have a quiet lunch and reserve one day of the week for all of the errands. I try to limit three evenings a week for events and appointments. I schedule at least one weekend of the month at home without leaving the house. Sometimes it is just one day of the weekend. I learned that if I don't plan my downtime, I will fill up the entire calendar slot! I have one day a week that I spend with my grandkids. And that is my favorite time of all!

So when Nick's accident happened, my life came to a screeching halt. There was nothing else I could have done, wanted to do except be at that hospital every day. If you've ever been faced with a loved one's accident, injury or illness, then you know exactly what I mean.

A funny thing happened though. About two weeks before the accident, all of the appointments that were scheduled on my August calendar cancelled or postponed. Each and every one of them. I remember thinking to myself, "Does God want me to have this much free time?" As it turned out, He did. God knew.

During the first two critical weeks, my husband, Skip, was not permitted to visit Nick or even enter the burn unit because he had a staph infection on his leg. It was so difficult for Skip to stay away, but he would have never done anything to hurt Nick's recovery. We texted each other often, and Skip shed many tears. It was actually there in the hospital when I first started to text. I had avoided it up until then. I discovered that was the only way to communicate to Skip, David,

Marcy or anyone because the phones didn't work well. Thank God for the technology marvel that is texting!

The days began very early. I forced myself to eat a small breakfast before I went out the door. My day usually began at Nick's office. He had opened his own business the year before; and in order for the doors to remain open, he needed my help. There was also an army of volunteers ready and willing to lend a hand. And you know what was most phenomenal? They all did it with a genuine desire to help and would not accept compensation. If not for them, the job could never have been done.

After Nick's office, it was off to the hospital so I could be there by 8AM in case the doctor came in. I also wanted to be there in case Nick was scheduled for an early tub treatment. He usually slept a lot after the tub from all the meds. I stayed at the hospital all day. It gave Hallie the opportunity to go home, shower, have some alone time with the animals and to recharge her batteries. Hallie and I had lots of opportunities to talk, and we really leaned on each other.

I took a lot of Excedrin™. I tend to get headaches if I don't eat regularly, don't get adequate rest or if I'm especially stressed out. The last thing I wanted to deal with was to be incapacitated with a headache, so I took the Excedrin™ as a preventive. It is the only thing that really works for me, and I took a lot of it.

Note: Sadly, now that Excedrin™ is off the market, I have discovered Bayer Plus™.

I usually left the hospital around 8PM when visiting hours were over. I started leaving a little earlier once he stabilized after his surgeries. Once I got home, Skip, made sure I ate something. So many people were providing food, which was so appreciated.

Then I went to bed. I didn't fall asleep, but I knew my body needed to just rest. The next morning I did it all over again.

I also made sure that I took my vitamins. Ok, I have to confess. On day two I actually asked my brother, Jim, to get me some multivitamins and calcium. He called, asked what he could get me and that's what I requested. I knew I was in for a long haul, and I'd better strengthen my body in any way I could.

Everyone knows their own body's thresholds. You must honor these. What good would we be to the ones who need us most if we allow ourselves to get too run down? We are no good to anyone if we shatter.

Lesson Number Six: Grit-your-Teeth Determination

Have you ever been really determined about something? Think back to when you were sixteen and wanted that driver's license. You were determined that nothing was going to stand between you and that little card. In some cases you had to convince your parents you were ready for the responsibility. And you were determined that they see things your way!

I was determined to get Nick a Cabbage Patch Kid™ for Christmas the year he was four. He wanted it and most of the other kids in America wanted one too. I showed up at a local retailer about twenty minutes before they opened because I saw an ad that said the store had them. There was quite a crowd that morning. It never crossed my mind that we were all there for the same thing! That was my first experience in mass marketing plus a child's desire equaling being stuck in a throng of pushing, frenzied parents! I lucked out that day and got the boy Cabbage Patch Kid™ that Nick wanted. He named him Josh and I still have it saved for him to this day.

Nick was never short on determination. He played football all the way from the youth leagues through high school varsity. He was the team co-captain his senior year. He was a true leader and earned the special team award that was given to one player at the beginning of each new school year who worked the hardest during the offseason. He not only earned the respect of the other players but of the coaches as well.

What he lacked in height he made up for in attitude, hard work, perseverance, determination and exceptional spirit. Pardon my language, but Nick was one bad ass on the football field.

I've seen his determination since then in his work ethic, workout mindset and sheer will to get any job done that he sets his mind to.

So it shouldn't have been any surprise to me to witness it during his recovery from his burns. And I wasn't surprised. Yet I was amazed and so very proud. The extent of his sheer will, his absolute grit staggers me still.

How Nick approached this experience is a testimony to what determination can do. His outlook from the early days in the hospital, through the surgeries and into the recovery phase was focused on one thing. And that one thing was to do everything in his power that day, that hour, that minute to get him home to Hallie and back to his life.

Did he have times of despair? Of course, he wouldn't be human if he didn't. Did he ever wallow in self-pity or play the Why Me game? Not once.

Can you face your obstacles with that mindset? Will you at least try?

Lesson Number Seven: Gratitude with Forgiveness—The Most Important of All...

Gratitude and abundance go hand in hand. To have an abundant life, we have to first be grateful for what we have. And we have to thank God for our many blessings each and every day. It is very easy to skip over this step and begin our days with a flurry of activity. But if we make it a point to make it a habit to be grateful, it will become a natural part of our day, of our mindset.

The easiest way to get ourselves into the Gratitude Habit is to use a Gratitude Journal. Then use it either first thing in the morning or the last thing at night. If another time of day works better for you, than by all means use that time. Record the things you are grateful for each day. At first they might include what you might expect, things like health, family, food on the table. But as you continue this exercise what emerges will be something different, something much deeper. It could be something as small as a smile from a stranger you pass, someone holding the door for you as you struggle with packages or even an unexpected compliment. These things will bring a smile to your face, joy to your heart and sunshine to your day.

Recently I had a full day of errands ahead of me. I had begun the day at 7AM with a doctor appointment and had the beginnings of a screaming headache. I knew I needed to eat something so I could take some aspirin, so I pulled into an area restaurant. As I prepared to enter the drive thru lane, I pulled out of the way so another car could get by me so I could look into my wallet to make sure that I had enough money. Since I had $4 and change, I thought "What the Heck!" I pulled back into the drive thru lane and placed my order for a breakfast sandwich and bottled water. When I got to the window, the cashier smiled at me and said the person in front of me had paid for my order! You can imagine my shock. First I didn't even know if I had enough money to even enter the drive thru line, so I let another car go ahead of me while I checked my wallet. Secondly, if I hadn't pulled out of the way, I would not have been the recipient of the Good Samaritan! So without any hesitation I paid the person's bill that was behind me. That experience put a glow on the rest of my day.

Simple acts of kindness. We are all capable of them. Go visit someone who lives alone. Take food to someone who has been ill. Send a handwritten card to a friend you haven't seen in a while. Do some chores or run some errands for someone who can't do it themselves.

Go through closets and drawers and donate usable items to your local Domestic Violence Shelter or other charitable organizations. Pull some items out of your pantry, and donate them to your church food cupboard. Give the person in front of you in the check-out line at the grocery store the twelve cents she's digging to find. Hold open a door. Smile at a stranger.

When Nick was in the hospital, the simplest smile from a stranger did wonders for me. It showed me that in spite of how busy the world is, a perfect stranger cared enough to smile at me.

That first day after the accident when I was crying so hard entering the parking garage that I didn't see where you got the ticket, the booth operator was so kind. She came out of the booth, retrieved the ticket for me and gently handed it to me with kindness in her eyes. And I was so grateful.

Everyone surrounding us has been so kind and loving. From storming the heavens with prayer to putting Nick's name on countless prayer chains these friends and family members were our rock. They fed our bodies and our souls. They kept up Nick's spirits with their messages to our blog and boosted us up along with him. Thank you didn't even begin to cover it. At a time when everyone including us felt helpless, people found a way to reach out. We felt their love, we felt protected through their prayers. We learned to give thanks in everything.

It is a humbling experience to be on the receiving end of so much from so many.

I learned that with Gratitude comes **Forgiveness**. After the accident, I discovered that I had been harboring anger toward a number of people based on past events. I had been wronged and I was left with hurt feelings that had grown into angry ones. I had even refused to patronize several businesses. I had justified my feelings as being righteous when in fact they were anything but. The truth is I didn't recognize in myself the feelings of anger that I often counseled others about. Wow! What an eye opener.

Every single one of these men and women reached out to me and my family during our time of need. In a quick rush of emotion, I realized with absolute clarity that I was the one who had been hurting needlessly all of this time. Those feelings brought me to my knees, and I felt ashamed. I felt humbled.

At that second I released my pent-up feelings and forgave everyone for what had happened. More importantly, I forgave myself.

I vowed that never again would I carry on my shoulders feelings of hostility, anger or hurt toward anyone. It felt so good to be completely free of all of that!

As each day goes on, I refuse to allow myself to go down that path. I won't carry into my future grudges or angry thoughts and feelings as I did learn the lesson of what forgiveness can do.

LIFE'S TAPESTRY

6

There is a wonderful poem by an unknown author called Life's Weaving. It is about the trials and tribulations we all experience in life and the deeper meaning of everything that we go through:

LIFE'S WEAVING
(Author Unknown)[23]

Life is but a weaving
Between my God and me;
I may not choose the colors,
He knows what they should be.
For He can view the pattern
Upon the upper side,
While I can see it only
On this, the under side.

---

23 *Life's Weaving*, Author Unknown, http://allpoetry.com/poem/4898791-Lifes_
Weaving__Author_Unknown_-by-Katie_Lazette

Sometimes He weaveth sorrow,
Which seemeth strange to me;
But I will trust His judgment,
And work on faithfully.
'Tis He who fills the shuttle,
He knows just what is best;
So I shall weave in earnest
And leave with Him the rest.
At last, when life is ended,
With Him I shall abide,
And I may view the pattern
Upon the upper side.
Then I shall know the reason
Why pain with joy entwined,
Was woven in the fabric
Of life that God designed.

I love that poem because it expresses better than anything I've ever read the fact that our lives are but a part of the grand design of God's plan.

Do you catch yourself getting caught in the If only trap? On the day of the accident, Nick was going to come over to my house to finish up some landscaping. That morning he called me and changed that plan saying he had some work he needed to get done on his boat. He said he would do the landscaping on the following day. At the time I didn't think anything of it. Afterwards I played the If only game. If only I would have insisted he come that day, then he wouldn't have been working on his boat that fateful afternoon! If only we had known that an empty gas tank holds more vapors than a full one! If only...

The early days of the accident are a blur to me now. A blur of pain and tears. I was definitely living in the moment as my mind couldn't comprehend the full scope of what was ahead. All of us were lifted up in prayer and comfort by so, so many. We felt cherished.

It is hard to calmly tell yourself in the midst of tragedy and disappointment that all things happen for a reason. And it would be even harder to say those words to someone who is going through a life-shattering event. But I believe those words with all of my heart. While I would never say that to someone else going through something similar or even worse than what we went through, I would think it. And I would pray to God to give that family courage to face what was in their future.

I have also learned through my experiences that I need to let go of worry. God doesn't want us to worry at all, but rather to give our trials and tribulations up to him. We need to trust him enough to do that. That is the ultimate life lesson.

As humans we want all the answers all of the time, and we want them right now. That is where patience and faith come into play. Patience that we must go through whatever it is that we are going through gracefully and maintain the faith that we are being held in the hands of God.

I don't understand how those without faith get through hardship. Their hearts must be so full of pain, depression and despair. We all need to pray for them and to our Lord to shine his light into their lives and hope that they will ask for his help. That's all they have to do, just ask. While the situation being dealt with won't just go away, God will hold you up so you can endure.

Good things do come out of tragedy. While that road isn't the one any of us would choose, we are made stronger by adversity.

Look to the example set by Christopher and Dana Reeve, Michael J Fox and John Walsh to name just a few. For each of them there are countless others. They took the experience that life dealt them, accepted it and did something worthwhile with it.

We all know Christopher Reeve for the role he played as Superman. But what we will all remember him for is the courage and grace with which he faced life as a quadriplegic after his accident while horseback riding. He was 42 years old. His wife, Dana, never wavered in her love for him. She treated him with love and respect and was a role model for their son, Matthew, and the world.

He formed the Christopher Reeve Foundation for spinal cord research and those living with paralysis. Imagine how many lives he has touched!

When Christopher Reeve died at the age of 52, followed by Dana less than 18 months later from lung cancer, the world was stunned and saddened. The Foundation, now called Christopher & Dana Reeve Foundation, is devoted to research for treatments and cures for spinal cord injuries.

In Christopher and Dana Reeve's case, their lives were changed in one instant and were never the same again. Of course they didn't ask, plan or wish for such a thing to happen. But when it did, they accepted it and looked for ways they could be useful. They found their purpose in life. And when their purpose was complete, God took them home.

Michael J. Fox is a much-loved actor. But I think what defines him in everyone's mind is his grace and attitude since his diagnosis of early onset Parkinson's disease. It is because of his total acceptance of the disease and the accompanying ongoing march of destruction that it will take upon his body that he is so admired. He is responsible for the Michael J. Fox Foundation for Parkinson's Research that has funded millions in research dollars for the quest for a cure and improvement in the treatment for Parkinson's disease. It is the most common neurological disease after Alzheimer's Disease. Over 1 million people in America have Parkinson's disease. About 60,000 Americans are diagnosed with

Parkinson's disease every year, and only 4% are under the age of 50.[24] Those are heartbreaking statistics.

My husband was diagnosed with Parkinson's Disease in 2008 at the age of 49. As the wife of someone living with Parkinson's disease, I am awed by Michael J. Fox and what he has accomplished. This is another example of life's purpose, and he speaks about it in his books. He has touched so many lives through his illness. He actually says that had he not gotten this disease, he would never have had the opportunity to serve.

Many times survivors of great disasters go on to accomplish things they never would have if they hadn't gone through the horror they faced. And they touch many lives. They turn lives around, and they make a difference to hundreds of thousands of people — or just one. That is purpose.

Do you remember little Adam Walsh? He was kidnapped while shopping with his mother in Florida and was later found decapitated. His father, John Walsh, later became an advocate for missing children and founded the well-known television show, America's Most Wanted. As a direct result of his efforts through his mission, over 1100 fugitives have been captured.[25] This is a prime example of a horrific event changing the lives of countless others.

While most of us won't go on to become famous because of adversity, all of us have the opportunity for growth and service from having endured our tragedies. But how? Exactly how do we know just what it is that we are supposed to do?

I can tell you this. Listen to your heart. Follow your inner urging that prompts you to move in new directions. Don't let the negative emotions overpower you.

---

24 Parkinson's Disease Foundation, Statistics on Parkinson's Disease, http://www. pdf.org/en/parkinson_statistics
25 Americas Most Wanted, Statistics on fugitives captured, http://www.amw.com

Think about exactly what you would be doing in life if money was no object. Then create a detailed plan to take steps necessary, one step after another, to live your dream. If you're afraid of hard work, then this exercise is probably not for you. But if you're willing to do what it takes to accomplish your goal, there is nothing stopping you but that first step toward your dreams.

After Nick's accident, and even during the ordeal, we were struck by how many different people shared with us their belief that Nick survived this accident for a reason. They shared on the blog, they shared in cards and letters and they even shared during phone calls and visits. The theme was the same. Nick had a purpose to fulfill that was only brought about by this accident.

He inspired so, so many by his attitude, serenity and determination each and every day. He strived to work even harder than what was expected to regain his life back. Each bite, each movement, each step was answered in grateful thanksgiving. He became a role model. This alone could be life's purpose, to change the course of another's life.

Yet I believe there is more. Nick has a natural magnetism about him. He's had it since he was a little boy. His smile got him free salad bar from the waitress during our beach trip when he was only four. The same smile got him free fries from a vendor at Cedar Point when he was ten. His natural, boyish charm shone through then, and still does now that he is a man.

I believe that this story has the potential to touch so many more lives, beyond the scope of his family and friends. I think it can be a source of encouragement for many. What follows from here is all in God's plan…

PHOTOS

Above: The aftermath of the fire

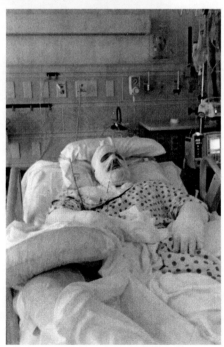

Right: Nick shortly after the accident

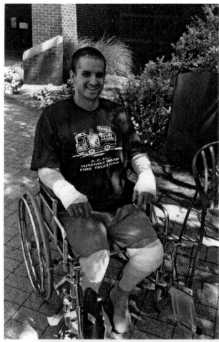

Enjoying the sunshine at the hospital after the surgeries were over

Nick & Hallie celebrated their 2nd wedding anniversary while he was in the hospital. This picture is from that happy day. From left: Nick, My older son, David, Hallie, David's wife, Karrie, My daughter, Marcy

The Bake Sale

*Presenting Nick with
the "Josh Cribbs"
autographed football*

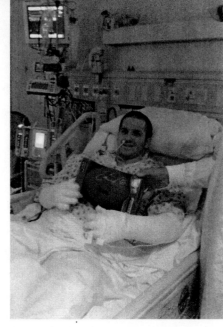

120 golfers turned out for the Golf Outing Fundraiser

Nick takes the first swing

Nick speaks at the Pasta Dinner Fundraiser

*The family at the Pasta Dinner. From left: Hallie, me,
Nick, My husband, Skip, Skip's mom, Norma*

The Amish "Garage-Raising"—Before

The work begins!

And the work continues...

The first roof truss goes on!

I loved watching those trusses fly through the air!

Busy little bees continue their work

Nick grills hamburgers for the workers

Hallie organizes the lunch buffet

*A few of the workers: From left, David,
Nick, Jesse Miller, AJ Geyser, Chris Miller*

Finishing touches

A Labor of Love

Nick and his company van

The grandkids: Ruby, Clayton, Brady, Grace

Nick and Hallie with little Brady

AFTERWORD

Almost two years have gone by since the accident. Nick is 100% and can do anything and everything he wants to do. He snow skis, water skis, swims, works out and tinkers with his cars. He cooks, cans, plants a garden and is very handy around the house. He and his wife also do a lot of traveling.

Nick has healed, but the scars are there. He has to be especially careful to wear sunscreen, but he can still enjoy the sunshine. His body's cooling system is forever out of whack, so when he overheats the sweat will pour from his head.

His business, Advanced Fulfillment Solutions LLC, is doing well and he employs some part time workers to help him with the workload.

The biggest change in their life was the happy and blessed birth of their first child in August 2011.

ACKNOWLEDGEMENTS

My heart is full of never-ending joy and thanksgiving to our Lord and Savior for laying His hands on Nick when he needed it most. I firmly believe this book is all part of His Plan.

Thank you so very much to David Hancock and my team at Morgan James Publishing: Margo Toulouse, Bethany Marshall, Jim Howard, Rick Frishman, David Sauer, Cindy Sauer and everyone who worked behind the scenes. Special appreciation to Michael Ebeling for the introduction! Because of all of you, the story of The Nine-Week Miracle will be heard.

I am thankful to the Akron Children's Hospital Burn Unit Staff for their wonderful care of Nick throughout his hospital stay and recovery period. Our gratitude to Dr Mark McCollum for his skill, compassion and kindness leading up to and during those four skin graft surgeries is impossible to express.

Our very large network of supporters sustained us during the crisis and beyond. Family, friends and complete strangers wrapped their arms around us and refused to let go.

About the Author

Photo by Julie DiTommaso

Maryanne Shaw has 19 years of marketing and writing experience. She is a successful ad copywriter covering topics from spirituality to natural health. As *Nick's mom*, she is the voice of *The Nine-Week Miracle*. Her book, *Angelwhispers: Listen for them in Your Life* was written under the pen name, Marcy D Nicholas. Schedule Maryanne to speak for your group or event. She and her husband, Skip, live in Ohio.

For more information visit **www.maryanneshaw.com**

CPSIA information can be obtained at www.ICGtesting.com
Printed in the USA
BVOW032101270113

311630BV00002B/9/P